Ed + Fonda

Thanks for your

support ~

God bless you

Wael Foley

THANK MY LUCKY SCARS

A Memoir

Ward Foley, Ph.D.*

*Physically Disabled

*Author of *God Didn't Make Me A Woman Because I Had Enough Problems*

ForWard Publishing
Norton, Kansas

Thank My Lucky Scars: A Memoir
© 2006 by Ward Foley

Author's Note: I have changed the names of some people in my story, and also, occasionally, the sequence of events. I have a responsibility to protect the confidentiality of my hospice patients and their families. Besides, I live in a very small town!

For information, contact:
ForWard Publishing
P.O. Box 3
Norton, Kansas 67654
785-874-5135
wardfoley.com
thankmyluckyscars.com

ISBN-10: 0-9789008-0-4
ISBN-13: 978-0-9789008-0-9

Cover design: George Foster, www.fostercovers.com
Book cover text: Write to Your Market, Inc.
Advisor: John C. Foley
Editing: Kathy K. Grow, DoWriteEditing, Yankton, SD
Interior design & typesetting: Liz Tufte, www.folio-bookworks.com

I could dedicate this book literally to thousands of people who, in my village, raised a pretty good child. If I just thanked all those who have helped me, the book would be full of names—and finished. However, I realize a book filled only with names might not appeal to an avid reader. So here I will simply thank God, my mother and father, and my wonderful wife.

CONTENTS

PREFACE

Since finishing my first book, I have tried to find a professional writer to tell my story. Hundreds of prospects and more than twenty years later, I still couldn't find the right person. Finally, it became apparent to me that I was supposed to write it myself.

No matter how well someone knows me, my style is my style, and reflects my life, where I've been, and who I am. Realizing that, I felt God wanted me to peck away at the computer and do my best to tell my story of love. To tell the story of a man who can't write but wrote two books. To tell the story of a simple man made simpler. To tell the story of how tragedy can turn to triumph. With God's help, the words came pretty easily—although the typing took forever.

The parts of the book that are really good are inspired, while the other parts are mine.

While writing this book, I had two friends read the first few chapters, then asked their opinions. The first friend said, "It is very good, although it doesn't flow real well." The second friend said, "It is very good and flows very nicely." I laughed, knowing I would never be able to please everyone, and that that wasn't the objective. I realized an autobiography, especially mine, will never really flow. This is about life, and when has life ever flowed?

THE ACCIDENT

The late fall air was cool as I sped along the highway, my thoughts alternating between gratitude for a recent visit with an old friend and all-too-familiar feelings of unrest and inadequacy. The traffic light turned yellow, and the car in front of me slowed to a stop. I stopped, too, and glanced in the rearview mirror.

My heart began pounding in my throat and my eyes stayed glued to the mirror as I watched a speeding truck weaving from lane to lane. It was not going to stop before it hit me.

With both feet, I pushed on the brake pedal with every ounce of strength I could muster, and then did something I had never done before —lay down across the passenger seat. "Oh Jesus, help me," I prayed as I waited for the impact. They always tell you, in moments of crisis, time seems to stand still, and it certainly did for me that day.

Finally, however, came sounds of metal on metal and screeching brakes. I felt my head bounce off the dash and hit the windshield, and a shower of shattered glass rained over me. My car skidded and finally slid to a stop. When the noise lessened and movement ended, I figured I was still alive, or at least conscious on some level, conscious enough to think,

"I'm going to die here, eight hundred miles from home, alone, far from my family."

My breathing was getting more difficult, and I could feel a moist warmth running down my face. Suddenly, I panicked. I began praying as fast as I could: "Our Father, who art in heaven, hallowed be Thy name. Thy kingdom come. Thy will be done . . . ," feeling somehow the more prayers I said, the sooner help would arrive.

Still praying, I began climbing out through a broken window. Two young men were headed toward my car. Thinking they were coming to help, I felt hope overcome me. However, as I watched, they walked away.

"Why did they leave and not help me?" My mind was flooded with fear. "I really don't want to die, God. Please help me. I am so far from home and all alone. Please, don't let me die."

Staggering to the side of the road, I sat down, leaning over, with my right elbow resting on the curb. Dazed and spitting blood with every breath, I prayed, "I have been through so much. Lord, please help me."

Suddenly I knew I had no control over this outcome. Although I was the most frightened and scared I had ever been, I was beginning to accept my own death. Lying on the side of the road, bleeding from what seemed to be everywhere, I continued praying.

"Forgive me for my sins. If I am going to die, then okay, but make it easy, please. This breathlessness isn't any fun."

Then screams and distant sirens became background for thoughts of my childhood. In my twenty-four years of life, I had faced death many times, but this would be a strange conclusion. My parents had fought for so long to make me feel normal. Now, having survived more than thirty surgeries, how much more normal could I be than to die in a car wreck?

SCARS SO FAR

I began my lifelong fight to be "normal" in Sacramento, California, where I was born—with clubfeet and clubbed hands, and without hip sockets and many muscles and tendons. I had struggled to do nearly everything, including staying alive at four months old when I developed staphylococcus pneumonia. I was saved by a new type of penicillin and the antibiotic chloramphenicol.

My hands were stiffly bent at the wrist and resembled short golf clubs. When I learned to walk at a little over two years old, I did so wearing braces made especially for me. My knees were also stiff and they barely bent, causing me to hobble. This, and my arms swinging back and forth as my body hunched forward, gave my movements a jerky, disconnected appearance.

Wearing braces twenty-four hours a day was very difficult. They were uncomfortable, heavy, and awkward, and their leather straps, tied around my calves, itched constantly. I scratched my legs until they bled.

I hated wearing the braces to bed and learned how to take them off at night and position them perfectly next to my feet under the covers so my parents wouldn't notice I didn't have them on. I thought I was pretty sneaky until years later, when my mom said she had known and had just wanted me to have occasional relief.

At four, I began preschool at Starr King Exceptional, a school for kids with special needs. The next year I was in kindergarten with the so-called normal kids. My teacher was Miss Venables, a former Miss California, and my mom always said she had never before seen so many dads attend parent-teacher conferences. In Miss Venables's class I learned how to tie my own shoes and was rewarded with a sucker, making it an important and memorable day.

Though I struggled throughout my life with trying to be normal, my parents always treated me just like my older brothers, Kirk and Craig, and younger brother, Chris. (Although, when chores needed to be done, I thought they treated me too normally.)

PLAY BALL

I loved sports, and started playing Little League baseball, braces and all, at eight. I was so excited and proud just to be one of the players. I obviously couldn't run as fast, or throw as hard, but I always played my best, and as much as anyone, only later learning the coach had to put each of us in for three innings. But I was really pretty good, batting over .400 throughout my Little League career. Although I looked different from the other kids, baseball made me feel normal and part of a team.

One afternoon, I stood on the sidewalk, watching all my friends play football on neighborhood lawns. (As usual, my brothers wouldn't let me play this rougher game.) The quarterback shouted, "10-24-62-hike," the ball shot back, the pass was in the air, going, going, and then gone . . . right through a neighbor's window. Well, at that point, everyone scattered for cover—except me, stuck not far from the scene of the "crime." I tried to run, but with twenty pounds of braces holding you back, you don't get very far very fast.

The front door opened and the gentleman stood with his hands on his hips. "Who did this?"

I've had many revelations in my life, but few loom as large as this one. No one else would ever be there to answer for me, or take the fall. So I did the only thing a strong, God-fearing youngster could do. I ratted.

Yes, I gave every name and where everyone was hiding. As each name was pronounced, the perpetrators slowly emerged from their hiding places and confessed.

My mother and father had taught me about Jesus since the day I was born. Later, whenever I read the "footprints in the sand" poem, about how Jesus carries us in our times of need, I wondered why He didn't carry me a little faster the day the window broke.

Still lying on the curb waiting and wondering if I was going to live or die, the distant sirens were becoming louder as help was getting closer. I had dealt with so much and now, this car wreck. I was bleeding from what seemed to be everywhere, still praying and reflecting on my life of twenty-four years.

DOING GOOD AND BEING BAD

At thirteen, I walked twenty miles, and, at fourteen, bicycled forty, and thus raised more than $1,000 for the March of Dimes. This was money that could help others, but, more important at my age, I won a trip to Disneyland the first year and a minibike the next. People would sponsor my best friend, Andy, at ten cents a mile and me at one dollar. At first I was bothered because they were judging me by the way I looked. Then I realized I would make more. So I happily took their dollars on my way to winning the top prizes.

That minibike was the greatest thing I ever won, but I learned quickly why my parents never wanted me to have a motorcycle.

Within a few weeks, Andy and I had built a wooden ramp in the backyard, found some old milk crates, and began jumping them. I jumped two, three, then four.

"I'm just like Evel Knievel," I said. Andy then suggested I try jumping five.

"I barely made four; five would be crazy."

"C'mon, you can do it. Just take a couple laps in the backyard to build up enough speed."

Reluctantly, I agreed.

Andy rooted me on as I took a few laps and headed for the ramp.

"Give it all the gas it's got," Andy yelled.

I turned the throttle as far as I could as I approached the ramp. My hands gripped the handlebars when I hit the air.

"I'm going to make it," I screamed, and I did. Only I forgot to let up on the gas and took off even faster when I again reached the ground.

At full speed I was heading straight toward a wooden fence, twenty feet from where I landed, and my hands were frozen. I crashed through the fence and into the side of the neighbors' aboveground swimming pool. Hundreds of gallons of water poured over me and into our backyard, flowing down onto the patio and almost into our home.

I stood up, soaking wet, a little sore and stiff, with numerous cuts and bruises, but no broken bones. Overall I was fine.

Andy's first words were, "I knew you could make it," and he couldn't stop laughing once he knew I was all right. "Man, you should have seen that."

When I realized I could still walk, I began assessing the situation and just knew my parents were going to kill me. I was scared and already praying when the next-door neighbor walked out back to see his pool flattened and completely emptied, and thirty feet of the fence destroyed.

I begged, "Mr. Kern, please don't tell my parents. I will pay to have this fixed." I only had a couple of dollars; paying for this amount of damage would have taken me years. But I continued to plead with Mr. Kern until he said he would have to think about it for awhile.

One good thing about being disabled is, when I had hurt myself and couldn't walk very well, no one noticed. During dinner that evening, my dad asked my mom if she had seen the backyard. My heart skipped a beat as I continued to chew my food and avoided looking at either of them. "The fence in the backyard is down; it looks like the Kerns' pool broke and our patio is flooded." He continued, "If they think I am paying for part of the fence because of their pool, they're wrong."

Now I was really nervous and tried to finish eating as fast as I could. If my dad knew and was hoping I would say something, I was not. I was taking my chances.

Mr. Kern never said a word to me again about the fence or pool. So many loving and caring people have helped me through life, and he was one example—and not just because he fixed the fence and pool without ever telling my parents.

SO MANY SURGERIES

Surgeries were difficult, but they become a way of life when you average one nearly every year.

On my tenth birthday, I was in a hospital bed recovering from knee surgery. At 6:00 A.M., I phoned home to ask Mom when she was coming with my cake and birthday presents. "I'll be there soon," she promised. Later, I felt bad because, on the way to see me, Mom got a speeding ticket. The officer didn't seem to care she had a lot on her mind and a spoiled, ten-year-old handicapped boy in the hospital, begging her to hurry up.

Every surgery made me a little better, a little stronger, and life a little easier. My ankles, wrists, and left knee have been reconstructed. I have had pins, screws, and buttons placed in and on my body. I have had bones broken, not by accident, but by my doctors. I have had muscles transplanted and received numerous skin grafts, some of which have actually made for great entertainment. I now have trouble growing hair on my head, but do grow it on the palm of my left hand.

Having had so many surgeries, I felt I had already been through enough for a lifetime and, therefore, more bad things wouldn't happen to me. Yet, I learned early that, just because I had a lot of problems, I wasn't exempt from more.

I worked part-time at a local doughnut shop while attending college. One day, five minutes before my shift ended, I slipped and fell. Both hands, up to my wrists, went into the 400-degree fryer.

My doctor impressed upon my mother and me the importance of keeping my hands clean. The first time Mom poured water on the tissue of my burned hands, I screamed in agony. Never getting upset, she stayed calm, continued washing my hands, and tried to help me relax. These burns provided some of the worst pain I have ever experienced. I now have an understanding of, and great empathy for, burn victims.

Hundreds of miles away from home, I was nervous, scared, and all alone on the side of the road.

Suddenly, I heard a voice and looked up. "You'll be okay. There is an ambulance on the way, and they will help you." The middle-aged, fair-haired woman, dressed in white, took and held my right hand and sat down next to me on the curb.

I blurted out, "If I need CPR, let them know the muscles in my chest are gone."

Years earlier, doctors had taken my pectoral muscles and built me biceps. The rehabilitation was quite interesting since my mind still thought those muscles were in my chest. Thus, in the early days, I had to think one direction in order to make my arms move another.

For example, in order to bring my arm down when it was straight out to my side, I would mentally have to pull it downward, since its natural behavior was for my elbow to bend with my hand coming toward my face. This was bizarre, but the exercises went well, until the day came when I was struggling to pull my arm down and, suddenly, my hand smacked me in the face.

Still, before the surgery, I could barely lift a glass of water with both hands. Now I can lift several pounds with one arm.

I had dealt with all the surgeries very well. Seeing progress, realizing that each operation enabled me to look better and do more, helped me accept all the pain. Being teased, made fun of, and laughed at was more difficult. Feeling less a person because of others—and myself—was also very hard.

When I looked in the mirror, I had to like what I saw before anyone else would. Accepting my abilities and disabilities with a positive attitude was one of the hardest challenges I faced. A friend once told me that God does not give us a good life or a bad life; rather, happiness is a choice. God gives us life, and we make it good or bad. I was also taught by my parents to look for the good in things and focus on what I *can* do.

All this is much easier said than done.

SEEING MYSELF

When I was nineteen, my doctor gave my phone number to a couple whose son was born with the same condition I had—Arthrogryposis

Multiplex Congenita (AMC). They called, believing it would help Paul to talk to someone who had experienced and survived what he was going through. I agreed, and was actually excited because I had never before met anyone with the same condition.

Thirteen-year-old Paul came into the room, and I was struck by how different we looked. I thought, "Oh, he is so much worse than I am and obviously hasn't had the great doctors I have had."

Paul was a very nice young man, and we talked with my and his parents for awhile, and then he and I went out and talked some more. I felt sad for him, because I, in a sense, could feel his pain. Not his physical pain, but the years of emotional tension to come. It seemed to me the hardest years were between thirteen and the early twenties, and I was emerging from them. He was only beginning down the path. The difficulties with relationships, like girls who said they really liked me but only wanted to be my friend, and the emotional ups and downs every teenager experiences—compounded by the physical deformities that set us apart from others—would only worsen for him, while for me, they were subsiding.

I knew what he had to look forward to during high school and I was glad that, when he saw me, he saw someone who had "made it through." I hoped that helped him. I know Paul and his parents thanked us profusely for the chance to talk and find hope.

For all the help they seemed to feel I had given Paul, he gave me much more. I actually felt blessed in not looking much like him and being so much better off.

After they were gone my mother said, "Ward, he looks just like you. Isn't that amazing?"

"I don't look at all like that," I replied, a bit indignant.

"You are mirror images of each other," said my father.

This was the first time I had a glimpse of myself through other's eyes, and I was shocked and upset. I didn't like what I saw, especially the way I looked on the inside. For I realized that, no matter how much I had tried to convince myself I was normal, I didn't believe it. On the outside I may have appeared to be at peace with myself, but, on the inside, I wasn't.

However, while trying to help Paul, I also discovered a need to help others. Not until much later would I realize how this desire to help others was going to help me.

THE FIRST BOOK

Immediately after meeting Paul, I decided to write a book. It took me many attempts, but finally I completed *God Didn't Make Me A Woman Because I Had Enough Problems*. When my mother asked about the title, I explained, "Mom, you and Grandma both worked full-time jobs and took care of the family, and I couldn't have done it all." Although I chose the title because I thought it was catchy and funny, I truly believed what I told my mother.

That book was both an endeavor to help others and to explore my own feelings about my life, but I knew I wasn't the greatest writer. In fact, I had to agree with most of a newspaper book reviewer's less-than-positive assessment. However, I felt he had missed the point when he said my writing skills were as clumsy as the way I walked!

Funny thing though. That didn't upset me; instead, it only reinforced my belief that what I was doing—trying to help people understand handicaps—was important. With that purpose and that accomplishment, I finally felt I was heading in the right direction.

At this moment, though, I was lying by the road, waiting for help.

THE LADY IN WHITE

I was not waiting alone, however. The lady in white, sitting with me on the curb, holding my hand, said, "I know it is scary, but I'll stay with you. Is there anything I can do for you while we wait?"

Her presence seemed familiar, and brought calm; I was glad to have someone with me. I was aware of a fair amount of confusion, but my hold on consciousness must have been limited because I couldn't seem to focus long enough to determine the cause of it. I could hear sirens in the background, and the lady in white told me emergency vehicles would arrive soon.

"Is there anything I can do for you?" she again asked.

I hated the thought of my mother finding out. She had worried for so many years about me, and now this. My work on my just-finished book had brought an even greater closeness between us, and, by most standards, we had already been very close. She had written as a preface to my book, "Words can say so little when someone's done so much. Ward will never walk alone. Bless you for being you . . . ." I knew her so well and knew how much she was going to worry. The thought of her having to deal with this was almost unbearable. My dad would be strong for her, even with his own grief, but . . . .

"Call my Mom and Dad?" I asked after the ambulance arrived, and gave her their number. I wanted to ask her to tell them first that everything was okay, but I couldn't seem to form a sentence longer than four or five words.

"Just as soon as I can get to a phone, I will," she replied as the ambulance attendants walked up. I clutched her hand more tightly, as the paramedics checked me over. As they lifted me into the ambulance, the woman asked, "Do you want me to go with you?"

I don't remember if I nodded or said yes, but she got the message and soon we were in the wailing ambulance and on our way. Things at this point become rather hazy, though I remember my mouth filling with blood.

My next memories are of the hospital, and of mixed feelings, being both reassured that the lady in white could now call my parents and being afraid she actually would.

Then she came into the ER with the news that she couldn't get hold of my folks; the phone number I'd given her didn't work. From behind me she said, "I'm sorry I couldn't reach them, and I have to go now. You're going to be all right, and they'll take good care of you." I couldn't see but could hear her, and I answered, "Thank you and goodbye." I was surprised at my sense of loss when the stranger left, but fear produces strange reactions.

My time in the hospital revealed a broken nose and numerous cuts and bruises. It also revealed the cause of the accident—a drunken truck driver with an alcohol level of .32. I was the first car hit, at more than forty miles per hour, and the next four vehicles were totaled. Everyone survived, but with injuries.

When I was released from the hospital, I decided to return home as soon as possible; however, there was one piece of unfinished business. I wanted to find the lady who had stayed with me.

My friend Sean and I hopped in his car, and our first stop was for a look at the accident report to see if she was listed as a witness. She wasn't. Folks in the emergency room didn't have a clue who she was, so we went next to the ambulance personnel. I hoped she had said something about herself that one of them would remember. It was very important to me to thank this woman, and I really did not want to leave until I talked with her. During the most frightening time of my life, she had stayed with me, bringing comfort and a sense of peace.

The ambulance driver said, "I'm sorry, but we would never let anyone ride in the ambulance with you. Anyone who would ride would have to do so in the front, and I can tell you we took no one with us on that run."

"You mean you don't remember her?" I asked.

"I mean, there wasn't any lady in white riding in the ambulance with you. We didn't see her and she wasn't with us," he said as he climbed into the ambulance for yet another run.

Suddenly I felt goose bumps all over my body. A beautiful fair-haired lady in white, bringing me comfort and peace? "Was it an angel?" I thought.

Other things began to make sense. I remembered, when I was lying on the side of the road, one of the first questions the paramedics asked was, "Who was driving the truck?" The lady in white had answered, but the paramedics, as if they hadn't heard a thing, asked me again.

When I had said goodbye to the lady in white in the emergency room, I now remembered the medical staff looking at me as if wondering to whom I was talking. Was I the only one who had seen this fair-haired lady dressed in white? Had God sent me an angel?

ANOTHER MEETING?

I got back into the car with Sean and explained the problem; as I did, I recalled that faint sense of familiarity accompanying her appearance by the side of the road.

Suddenly I remembered something from a time which seemed too early for memory, of when I was four months old and critically ill with complications from my birth defects and pneumonia. My parents told me, much later, they had been informed I would not survive.

The peace and calm the lady in white brought during my accident felt a lot like this memory of hovering in a corner near the ceiling of a hospital room, above the open door, looking down at a crib, in which was a small deformed baby. My parents were standing on either side of the bed. A nurse, at the end of the bed, was doing something to that little body—my body.

Now I remembered a lady hovering with me in the corner of the room. She said, "The choice is yours."

"What choice?" I asked.

"You may come with me, or you may stay and help them."

"Where would we go?" I remember asking, but, somehow, when I looked at my parents, I knew I would stay.

"It's beautiful," is all I remember her answering, but my heart felt a longing for my parents below.

"No, I think I want to go with them." I added a bit hesitatingly, "I think they need my help, and maybe I can do something to ease their pain." I then said, staring down at the child on the bed, "I can do that. I can be him."

We continued communicating, through thoughts, even though I describe them as words. I said again, "I can do that. I can be him."

My memory of the experience faded as Sean asked, "Are you with me or what?" His question pulled me back into the here and now, and into our search for the lady in white.

"Yeah, I just had a weird memory of a dream or something that happened when I was small. I think I've seen that lady before. I think she helped me one other time."

"Yeah?" he asked, a bit hesitant.

"Yeah, her presence," I replied. "That presence has helped me before. Her presence was so beautiful and peaceful. I can only say one thing for sure, Sean—the lady in white, whether a heavenly or an earthly being, to me was an angel." I knew God had carried me through the most frightening time in my life.

ON THE ROAD AGAIN

I restarted my efforts to promote my recently published autobiography as soon as I recuperated from the car accident—a recuperation which included nose surgery, physical therapy, and the healing of all my cuts and bruises.

During college, when I had been an intern at KCRA-TV in Sacramento, I was fortunate to meet someone who became a light for me. Anchorman Vince Gibbens encouraged me to tell my story and to stay involved in media work. His friendship gave me the confidence to reach for what sometimes seemed an impossible dream.

After he moved to Milwaukee to anchor the WITI-TV news, he invited me to come and stay with him and his wife, Christine, and their family for a couple of weeks. And he offered to line up some speeches while I was there, so I could share my story and sell my books.

I was thankful to Vince and excited to go, although a little nervous because I hadn't done many speeches. In fact, my first had come just a few months earlier.

A colleague of my mother invited me to speak at her Southern Baptist Church. I had grown up in a fairly diverse neighborhood; however, this was the first time I had been anyplace where I was in the minority. Sean and I were the only white people at the service. Not only that, but I had always been a Catholic and was very accustomed to "rehearsed responses."

The pastor told the congregation a bit about me and then introduced me as "Brother Ward." I wasn't very far into my speech when a voice shouted out, "Hallelujah!" I was startled, but kept my composure and continued my speech. Soon came another shout of "Hallelujah," then another, and then three people jumped up and, with waving hands, yelled, "Praise the Lord and hallelujah!"

"Wow," I thought. "This is going great." Praise the Lord and hallelujah were not forms of expression usually heard by a young Catholic man in the 1970s. It could not have been a better first experience.

When I arrived in Milwaukee for my first trip to the upper Midwest, Vince met me at the airport and arranged for me to rent a car. However, in my naiveté, I had failed to realize I would need a credit card for that purpose, and didn't have one. I gave Vince a "help me" look, and he responded with, "No problem." Then he arranged for me to drive a car rented on his credit card.

When he handed me the keys, he laughed and said, "Just don't wreck it!" I've probably never been so nervous driving any car before or since. I valued his friendship and held him in such awe that I couldn't imagine having to tell him I had wrecked a car rented in his name.

He and his family welcomed me into their home, and, that night, I fell into bed exhausted from the excitement as much as from the travel.

The next morning, Vince gave me about twenty ties. Having now lived in the Midwest, I think he might have been telling me there was a dress code for this part of the country, and I might be better received if I adhered to it. Later that morning a woman called to ask me what honorarium I expected. I hadn't a clue what she meant, and Vince must have sensed my problem as he whispered the definition to me. He was always willing to help, and never made me feel stupid.

That first afternoon, I did a talk show at a local radio station. About twenty minutes into the program, we began to take phone calls. Soon a woman called to say she had a very young daughter with AMC. Following the show, I talked further to Renee, and we made arrangements to meet.

The first time I saw her daughter Courtney, I was stunned. She looked so much like pictures of me at age three, and I was overwhelmed with memories and emotion. Now I was the same age as her parents, and it was painful to witness the hurt in their eyes. I got a glimpse of what my parents had seen, and realized in a new way how hard it must have been for them. Suddenly, everything I had gone through seemed easier than having to be a parent of someone with a disability.

I gave them one of my books and was so proud to be able to share my story of hope with them. What a feeling of satisfaction and validation to finally see the results of writing my book and traveling the country.

The following weekend I spoke at all the masses at a Roman Catholic church. My pro-life message promoted my belief in God's ultimate wisdom and purpose for my life. Not having an abortion because your child is handicapped was an important message. Where would I be had my mother aborted me? I believe a disability does not have to be the end of life; it can be the beginning.

After those speeches I received a request to speak at a local school with Milwaukee Brewers second baseman, Jim Gantner. We each shared our message of faith and then played catch on stage. My awkward movements made it a perfect example of how "unlike" does not mean "unable." I can do most of what others do; I may do it differently, but, nevertheless, I can get the job done. And, this time, I received my first standing ovation!

After the speech, Jim showed me around the area. I think he wanted me to experience things I might not have access to in California. Well, he did—ice fishing.

Now, my family is sports-minded, but they don't really acknowledge fishing and hunting as sports. That's country, and we're city. I can't explain, as I don't think I've ever really understood it, but that's just the way it is.

Meanwhile, it turns out ice fishing begins with driving out onto the lake, very disconcerting when you've lived all your life in an area that doesn't even see snow. I just knew the truck's weight would break the ice and in we'd go. Talk about stepping out on faith. Then we reached our destination—a shed on the ice, with no heat and no running water, where I sat, freezing to death, with dreams of California filling my head.

We then dropped our lines down a little hole in the ice. At the end of what seemed to be all day, we hadn't caught a thing.

And, in spite of the cold and my fear, I had a great time.

After a few more speeches, I headed home to Sacramento, taking with me many such good memories and leaving behind not even a single scratch on the rented car.

WHEELING INTO MATURITY

A pattern began to emerge in my mind as I spoke to various groups. As a typical teenager, I had focused on my own problems, but, as I encountered more and more people, I realized all problems were basically the same. Whether physical, emotional, or spiritual, only the tools we apply to them are different, and some tools are more successful than others. Using a hammer when you need a screwdriver just doesn't work.

I was maturing, but still retained the youthful idealism that both helps us get things done and encourages us to pursue impossible feats. And so began my plan to ride a bicycle from California to Alabama to visit my Aunt Mary Kay.

She had developed rheumatoid arthritis at thirty, and we share many of the same experiences. Throughout my life I have confided in very few people regarding my personal and emotional troubles, but Mary Kay was one in whom I did. I could talk to her anytime I needed, and always felt better after doing so.

Thus, it seemed the logical place for me to begin my endeavor to "save the world" was Alabama, home of my Aunt Mary Kay and Uncle Jack. I would bicycle up to their front door to say thank you to Mary Kay for all she'd done for me, but would also ride in hope of encouraging others and to try to show the importance of reaching for one's best every day.

Searching for our place in life is just part of being young. My unique challenges and my own struggle for acceptance magnified my search. Though at the time I thought I was headed in the right direction, I can now see I was headed in many directions.

I couldn't make the trip by myself, so began looking for the right person to accompany me. I had known Steve a long time, although not well, but we enjoyed each other's company and he was a registered nurse.

When I approached him, I did so in a way that surprised even me: "Steve, go with me on this trip, and you will truly see miracles and how God works in our daily lives." Although I always thought of myself as religious and a Christian, I really wasn't fanatical, and that sounded a bit fanatical to me. Despite my zealous approach, he agreed, and planning began.

The miracles began before I ever even got on the bicycle seat. I knew I needed a really good bike to make a trip like this, so I went to McConaha's Bike Shop, just a few blocks from my parents' home, hoping they would either have a good used bike, or would sell me a new one at discount. Instead, Mr. McConaha gave me an eighteen-speed bicycle, absolutely free, plus extra tires, cycling pants, and other supplies I might need. We were ready to go.

I intended to ride as much of the way as possible while acknowledging there would be certain areas too dangerous to try. Because of my active lifestyle, however, training went relatively smoothly, and soon we were preparing equipment, mapping our route, and getting ready to depart from southern California, east of Los Angeles.

The big day arrived, and I rode out onto the two-lane highway; Steve followed in the car.

Less than two hundred yards into the ride, a semi-tractor-trailer rig passed us, and the force blew me off a twenty-foot embankment. I rolled down the hill, bike and all. Fortunately, I am an experienced "faller," and that served me well that day! When I emerged from the drop-off, nothing was hurt except my pride. I know Steve thought, and was too kind to say, "This is going to be a long trip." It was also a good thing we had practiced speedy flat-tire repair because, that first day, we fixed two.

We weren't like sponsored bike riders. No, we were on our own, which, practically, meant we had little in the way of money. Our plan was to sleep in the car at local parks. The first evening we settled into one after an exhausting day and fell sound asleep. For a short while. Jolting us awake were sirens, flashing lights, and then a flashlight glaring in my face. Apparently, of all the parks we could have chosen, we had picked one in the worst part of town.

We drove around until we located a fast-food restaurant open all night. The manager said we could sleep in the parking lot. This time, just as we were dropping off again, I heard loudly over the restaurant intercom, "Welcome. May I help you?" We decided from then on we would park either at police or fire stations, or, when we thought we could afford to, stay in motels.

The first two days went pretty smoothly, but the third morning I could hardly bend my knees, and the rest of my body wasn't a lot better. I wanted to call Mary Kay, but, since the trip was supposed to be a surprise, I called home. Whenever I was down, my parents' voices always helped lift my spirits. I tried to sound upbeat, but I probably didn't succeed. I don't remember seriously thinking of quitting, but I did certainly wonder what I had gotten into.

The record day of the entire ride was a whopping (and, I must admit, throbbing) eighty-four Texas miles. I suppose I have to add that the wind was strong and at my back, and it was a flat landscape. Still it was eighty-four miles in one day!

Then there was Dallas. Remember, I had told Steve, if he came with me, he would experience miracles? Well, just getting as far as I had was a miracle for me, but now a miracle according to his definition was about to occur, one of the "God things" in my life.

When we rode through Dallas, a local television station did a story on my ride. I thought it would be neat to tape the piece and send it back to my family. So we decided to stop at a Radio Shack, in the middle of a city where we knew no one and no one knew us, to watch the program and ask the employees to tape it for us.

During the show, a man standing behind me said, with excitement in his voice, "Is that you on TV?"

"Yes," I answered.

"That's amazing. Wait here a minute. Don't go anyplace," he said as he turned and began to leave. "I'll be right back," he yelled.

Several minutes later he returned with his wife and ten-year-old daughter. After introductions, the gentleman said, "We had a son with arthrogryposis, and he died at a very young age. We've never known anyone else with the condition. I asked my wife and daughter to come meet you."

"Wow!" I thought. This was amazing! And sad.

We talked, and they invited us for dinner. It was surely a miraculous thing that, in all Dallas, we would stop at that Radio Shack, and this man would be there at the same time.

I mailed the videotaped news story back to my family in California. Kirk, my oldest brother, was watching the video late one evening when he noticed his seven-year-old daughter, Megan, crying in the kitchen, where, unknown to him, she had been watching, too. When Kirk asked her what was wrong, she said, "Daddy, I didn't know Uncle Wardie was a handicap." Looking back, I can see how accepting a little girl was of her uncle, who had not been nearly as accepting of himself.

The next day we were off again. The day was clear and I was pedaling smoothly down the highway. About mid-morning, a car drove by us in the opposite direction, then slowed to a stop, turned around, and headed back our way. The car pulled over and stopped about two hundred feet in front of me. I was a city boy, so you can imagine my thoughts.

The car doors opened slowly on each side. I stopped pedaling and began coasting, all the while getting more nervous. However, when two ladies in their mid-seventies climbed out of the car, I was relieved. Even I could outrun them! Turns out they had seen the newscast on television, and thought what I was doing was wonderful. They each handed me one dollar. I've had few things in my life touch me like that. The rest of that day was an easy ride.

ARRIVAL

Throughout the trip, we called my cousins to make sure my aunt was not watching the news, as my greatest wish was to surprise her. As we approached Tuscaloosa, she still had no idea.

Others, however, knew. Cars honked and people waved as I rode through town. I was ecstatic, and thankful, as I approached the final few blocks. Two police officers on motorcycles led the way, while another followed. A news reporter knocked on Mary Kay's front door, and asked her to step outside. When she did, the reporter pointed to me riding up to her house, then told her I had just ridden my bicycle across the country for her.

I got off my bike, and we embraced one another while her five-year-old son, Michael, ran up and hugged my leg. Aunt Mary Kay was shocked and excited to see me. She couldn't believe what I had accomplished, and neither could I. I had done what I hoped; I had done my best every day.

After a few days of rest, Steve and I headed back to California, making one stop in Texas so I could give a speech at the school attended by the ten-year-old girl I'd met through our Radio Shack miracle. The classroom was packed with kids in chairs and all over the floor. The little girl's eyes told the story; she was so happy for me to be sharing my experiences with her friends.

I spoke for about thirty minutes, and the children asked questions for another thirty. The questions were more entertaining than my speech. One young boy asked, "When you rode your bike across the country, did you ever cut across the neighbors' lawns?"

I arrived home just in time for Christmas with my family. A local news reporter, Jonathon Mumm, did a very nice story about my ride, even interviewing Mr. McConaha, giving him some recognition for all he had done for me. Without his bicycle, and all the other supplies, I could never have accomplished the trip. My friend Vince Gibbens had made numerous calls to set up the police escort and television coverage. And Steve got me to Alabama safely. There simply were no words then— or now—to describe my appreciation or love for all the work they put into making my dream a reality.

A LONG RIDE

I had long ago labeled AMC, "*my* condition." Now, however, I had met Paul and Courtney and the Texas family whose son had died. The fact that none of these families had ever encountered anyone else with AMC, and I hadn't either until the day Paul and his family visited, sparked my interest in finding still others.

It is hard to put into words how I felt whenever I did, and what these families gave to me. I know now I was searching for personal answers; at the time I only knew I definitely was being drawn toward others with my condition. I decided to travel the country and find families with AMC children. I felt just meeting them would be enough. Nothing spectacular needed to be done.

I started back in Texas, where the family I had met on the bike ride awaited my arrival. The mother had been contacted by a few others after seeing my story on the news. From there, I headed to Alabama to stay with Aunt Mary Kay.

Two hours from her home lived a twelve-year-old boy with a much more severe case of AMC than mine. He moved his wheelchair by blowing in a straw-like tube. I felt horrible for him, although he didn't want me, or anyone else, to do so. He had the greatest attitude, and we became very close for the short time we spent together. His parents were wonderful, and they invited me back the next Sunday to speak at their church. The small congregation listened intently as I told my story. The talk went very well, but, more important, I had a great new friend.

God always seemed to guide and take care of me, whether or not I was aware of it. Once, I was driving to Wisconsin when I realized a toll was coming, and I didn't have any money. I frantically searched the ash tray for change and found instead a fifty dollar bill. The family I had just visited in Illinois must have put the money into my car. At first I wasn't sure if this was a gift from God; then I looked more closely at the bill and read, "In God We Trust."

On another occasion, I got to meet a happy young boy who not only had AMC but Down syndrome. Even though he couldn't use his arms, he played a trumpet by holding the instrument with his feet and pushing the keys with his toes.

CELEBRITY FRIENDS

On my way back home to California, I stopped again in Texas, this time to meet Zig Ziglar, one of the greatest speakers I had ever heard. Years earlier, I had been privileged to talk to him for about a minute after one of his speeches. He said then, if I was ever in his area, to look him up. So I did. I am positive he didn't remember me, but no one would have known. Despite what was probably a bit of shock, he invited me in and made me feel like an old friend, taking me to morning prayers with his employees and then back to his beautiful office.

During an hour-long visit, he gave me great advice on speaking and my future, and told me, "You may not think you're a great writer or the best at speeches, but you are an excellent communicator." As I got up to leave, we shook hands, and in the palm of his hand was a fifty-dollar bill. "Keep in touch," he said. What a wonderful man. The money was a nice gesture, but it was the time he spent with me that was invaluable.

My next stop was Los Angeles, where a five-year-old spark plug looking like I had at his age awaited my arrival. Sammy was a huge wrestling fan and especially loved Hulk Hogan, whom he had met the previous month. Sammy couldn't stop talking about his hero.

I later met Hulk Hogan, too, through this family. We had our picture taken standing next to each other; luckily, I wore a hat that day so people could tell us apart.

I was reminded by this experience of my own childhood hero, Joe Namath. He had sent me autographed pictures and other mementos, and wrote me wonderful letters. Once, when he was in town making a movie, he actually contacted me so I could come see him.

After I finished my first book, I mailed a copy to Oprah Winfrey, who took time out of her busy schedule to write me the nicest letter of support. Joan Lunden, of *Good Morning America*, even called my home with words of encouragement.

Later, when Jay Leno took over *The Tonight Show*, I wrote reminding him of a brief encounter we'd had in Sacramento, during which I'd told him that, if he ever made it "big," he could hire me and thus fulfill his obligation to hire the handicapped. Now I asked if he had made it "big" yet. *Tonight Show* staff wrote back and said they had wanted to thank me personally, but had been unable to locate my phone number.

When my cousin Brian Cabral played for the Super Bowl Champion Chicago Bears, he introduced me to a number of his colleagues, including Jim McMahon and Coach Mike Ditka. All went out of their way to make me feel welcome.

While I was studying to be a sportscaster, Brian set up a meeting for me with Walter Payton so I could interview him on my ten-dollar tape recorder. I cherish that interview to this day. During my broadcast training days, Jim Gantner also arranged for me to interview Dave Parker and Tony LaRussa.

I came to know Ed Hearn, former major league catcher and author of *Conquering Life's Curves*, when I heard him speak about his struggles (as Ed says) "From the Penthouse to the Outhouse, and Back."

Following his speech, Ed invited me to join him for a soft drink, and we shared stories and laughs. I immediately loved his sense of humor. He told me my hands looked like those of an old catcher and tried to give me a high five. That was a sight to behold! Ed helped me so much with speeches and writing, but, most important, by being a friend. One can never have enough friends, especially smart-aleck ones with disabilities.

All these celebrities were very patient and helpful, and did their best to support me. Too many times we hear only the negatives, and not enough about the great things famous people do for others. But, whether I was meeting a child with AMC or a Super Bowl MVP, I tried always to remember they were equally "famous" in the eyes of God. The question was, did I believe that about myself?

A HARD RIDE

I'd now seen the excitement of many AMC families at the opportunity to meet someone else with the condition, and, having had more success bicycling across the United States than I ever expected, I decided to ride across Russia.

Steve and I went to the Soviet consulate in San Francisco to get permission. Since this was before the collapse of the USSR, we were both nervous as we entered through several gates under the watchful eyes of multiple cameras and security men.

The man who greeted us asked immediately what we wanted. I told him I hoped to go to Russia and ride my bicycle across his country.

"No," he said sternly, and that was about all we understood. He then sent us to a Russian travel agency several miles away. Why, we had no idea, since he'd said we couldn't do the ride, but we did as he said anyway.

A couple of blocks into the trip to the travel agency, I noticed we were being followed. We weren't sure if they were Russian or U.S. people, but they made Steve and me very nervous as they followed us all the way.

When we arrived, I told the travel agents I wanted to ride my bicycle across their country, and they laughed and said, "No way."

"Why?" I asked.

They answered none of my questions, but kept saying they just would not allow me to ride my bike across Russia.

On the way home, we kept an eye on the rearview mirror, but, as far as we could see, no one was following us. The whole trip felt like a waste of time, though, for a few days, I continued to plan ways to go to Russia.

Finally, an acquaintance—Margaret Larson, KCRA-TV anchorwoman—convinced me that riding across Russia was not a good idea, taking time to explain how different a country it was and how much trouble I could get into by going without permission. Thanks to Margaret, my plans changed, and I decided Canada would be much more open to the idea of me cycling on their soil.

I had been in contact with a Vancouver geneticist who had been instrumental in helping me understand the different kinds and severities of AMC. From her, I had learned that my condition was not genetic. Now, she put me in touch with numerous Canadian families whose children suffered from AMC.

I left from Vancouver in July, planning to arrive at Toronto in August. And, just as with the United States ride, this wasn't about miles ridden, but doing my best each day. I knew some days would be better than others.

Canada was truly beautiful, and the people were the same, supportive and encouraging throughout the journey, eh? (It took me months to quit saying "eh" at the end of my sentences.) I was able to meet many AMC children and their families.

Yet, the last few weeks of this ride became very difficult, physically and emotionally. The distance, the pain, and pure exertion were making me tired and frustrated, and everything seemed to be harder and take longer than it had when I'd ridden across the United States. I just couldn't pedal as much each day. In fact, I could barely ride at all. A few miles here and there were all I could do. I felt I was still doing my best, but I was disappointed.

I had hoped to end my ride in Exhibition Stadium during a Toronto Blue Jays baseball game with my hometown Oakland A's. Toward the end of the trip, I learned all they could do was announce my name during the game. Tired and extremely frustrated, mostly with myself, I finished the ride in an empty parking lot, with no fanfare, and headed home.

I realized I had thought I was riding to help others, but had really done it more for myself. I wanted to be something I was not; I was trying to be better—to be equal.

Though I'd been blessed by many loving and caring supporters throughout my life, I had also been teased and harassed. Many, many times, others had been mean and hurtful. For example, I was the equipment manager for my high school baseball team, which included a player who would imitate my walk while laughing. My hands were still curled under in those days, and he often chased me around the field, saying he was going to hang me on the fence. I tried to laugh it off. I asked him nicely, and in private, to quit, but every day he continued. I began to hate going to baseball practice, something I had always loved. I tried avoiding him at every turn because just seeing him made me nauseous.

When I encountered this type of person and similar embarrassing and hurtful situations, I often thought, "Someday, I'm going to be famous. Then everyone will like me."

By not letting others know how much pain this caused, I was also deceiving myself. Smiling and being happy on the outside may fool some people and even ourselves for awhile, but eventually it catches up with us. I thought I had already dealt with all these issues; now I was learning I would have to deal with them forever. That hard truth was depressing.

I'd been home from Canada less than two weeks when I was awakened in the middle of the night by extreme chest pain. I couldn't move. I lay on my back with my arms at my side, barely breathing, feeling as if an elephant were sitting on my chest. I tried to yell for my roommate, Don, but couldn't. My mind was screaming but nothing was coming out of my mouth.

"Oh, my God, what now?" I began praying, "Please help me, Lord!"

I tried again to sit up, to get out of bed, to shout, but nothing happened. Frozen stiff, I lay there helpless and scared.

Minutes that seemed like hours passed in fear and prayer before the pain subsided and I was finally able to get Don's attention. My doctor immediately put me in the hospital, where I was monitored in intensive care for several days. Though doctors thought I had had a heart attack, numerous tests showed, thankfully, that nothing was seriously wrong. I was just physically worn out and totally drained.

I was glad to leave the hospital and go home, but, otherwise, I felt only exhaustion and deep sadness. I was tired of helping others, was done trying to "save the world." I realized I needed now to save myself.

Most of my life I had been able to see the positive. Until now. Now I was focused on the negative, and mad at the world. Things began to bother me—childhood thoughts, relationships, pain caused by my condition. Suddenly the world was not fair. I knew my terrible attitude was wrong, but I didn't care. This change had sneaked up on me so quickly. I was emotionally drained and headed down, into depression.

In such a state, emptiness and sadness fill the gut, and it feels like there is no end to the sorrow. Nothing seems to help; no one understands. On the outside, everything looked fine; on the inside I was hurting emotionally, more than I ever had before. I couldn't even fake a smile anymore. This from a guy who had thrived on being happy—and on not letting anyone ever know how bad he could feel.

This pain was devastating and I couldn't seem to get over it by myself; I needed help. I even talked to Dr. Frank Boutin, my orthopedic doctor since within hours of my birth, though this he couldn't fix with surgery. Thankfully, I was at least able to recognize what was happening.

I remember stopping to see my mom one day just to say hello. Mom's office was, for me, a home away from home. Throughout my growing years, I had spent countless hours in her break room, before and after doctors' appointments. Her coworkers were like family. Whenever I didn't feel well, physically or emotionally, I knew I could stop at her office and feel special.

Mom always had known if I was troubled in any way. We didn't even have to talk about any specific problem; she just had a way of making things better. On this particular day, Mom told me how proud she was of everything I had done, and, especially, of who I had become. She said there was nothing wrong with seeking help if I felt depressed. I was relieved as I had thought that might be a sign of weakness. It meant so much to me to realize my mom understood.

I had already overcome so much. Or had I? Had I really dealt with the teasing and tormenting, and the feeling that I was somehow less a person? Or had I simply been ignoring things I needed to face? I had no answers, just more questions.

Especially I wondered why, when I met both celebrities and others with AMC, I truly felt they were all equal in the eyes of God, yet couldn't see myself in the same way. My seven-year-old niece had cried when someone called me handicapped; she saw me as "normal." Why couldn't I?

Thanks to my mother's wise and timely words, I decided to see a counselor. I knew now this was not about weakness, but an illness. We all have problems, and mine had simply come to a head at this time in my life.

ROCKY ROMANCE

I was now struggling in all aspects of my life but especially with dating. How, I wondered, could someone love me, looking the way I did? It didn't help when I had gone out with a girl four or five times, thinking we were getting serious, only to have her tell me during dinner, "I am sorry if I misled you, but I thought you knew I wouldn't date someone like you."

Of course, when someone did like me, I apparently couldn't believe that either. I had been engaged to a woman who called off the wonderful wedding we had planned when she decided she preferred someone else. I was so sad and hurt, and embarrassed. This only affirmed my doubts, and I became even more frustrated.

I did have one great relationship. Lynne, a high school friend, and I were like brother and sister. Whatever I went through would have been worse without Lynne's love, support, and understanding. Deeply compassionate, and the definition of a true friend, she took me to dinner one night and introduced me to one of her friends. Soon Lynne's friend and I were dating and having a great time. She was studying to be a social worker, and I always felt she could practice on me.

However, after awhile, the relationship ended because of my immaturity and insecurities. Somehow, I managed to mess up every attachment in which I was involved. I didn't do it on purpose, but I was usually the cause of the breakup. Whenever I had what I thought I wanted in a relationship, I couldn't believe it to be true. I began thinking, "When and how will this relationship end?" What I hadn't realized was, when someone agreed to go out with me, this meant they usually had already accepted my appearance.

During this time, even if the women I dated had been right for me, I probably wouldn't have seen it, or let it be. Wallowing in self-pity, being depressed, and not liking oneself makes it hard for others to like us, too.

I had met three of my closest friends—Sean, Don, and Patti—while working at Taco Bell, my first job, and we have continued our wonderful friendships through the years. Having such good friends, especially when times are difficult, is a gift.

Patti and I had even dated in the past; yet, after we quit going out, we remained friends. Now, sensing my pain, Patti sent me a poem she had written after we had broken up. I repeat—*after* we had broken up.

I met a boy who made me laugh
He was part of the team and fun to work with
He would make you feel strong by the stories he'd tell
His wit hides the pain his body knows so well.

I saw his scars and learned of his surgeries
He was born with inner strength that knows no boundaries
I tried to understand, feel his pain
But that was a place I had never been.

He wants to help people and follows that dream
He'll always be successful at everything
He draws, he writes, he motivates
Kids make him happy, and in life he has faith.

I know he will challenge himself forever
He considers me his friend, and that I will treasure
His eyes tell the story if you are fortunate enough to see
I was one of the lucky ones, in him I believe.

I still cherish this poem. Despite the end of our romantic relationship, Patti had seen through my disabilities and emotional struggles and deeply cared for me as a person. I still read this poem for comfort, especially in times of extreme struggle, sadness, or the kind of emptiness I knew during this time.

Looking back, I now realize that many of my dating and relationship woes were common. I thought my problems in such areas were because of my disability or appearance. And some were, but most were not.

Actually, reflecting now on those days, my disabilities gave me an advantage. I could always blame my problems with women on that, while the so-called normal person would have to admit he had a bad personality!

A TURNING POINT

With no definite direction, I continued taking classes, talking with a counselor, and hanging out with my supportive friends. One evening Steve and I sat in a restaurant eating pizza while reminiscing about the bike ride across the country. The conversation changed to talking about my frustrations, disappointments, and sadness, which led to a discussion about faith and God.

I was getting sad and upset. I told Steve I was doing my best in life, but it didn't seem to be good enough, at least not good enough for me. I had tried my whole life to be strong and courageous, to never give up. At the end of our meal and conversation, I sadly said, "Steve, I am trying to do my best."

He then said three words, referring to God, that I will never forget: "He knows it."

These words came out of Steve's mouth, but in a totally different voice. Chills went up my spine as if I were hearing a message from Jesus Himself, as if Jesus totally understood my frustrations and was letting me know everything would be all right—I just had to keep trying.

Although very different from my experience following the car accident, this too was powerful. I was instantly calmer and more relaxed, and again felt God helping me through a tough time. I suddenly had a glimmer of hope.

Steve and I went back to my apartment and talked about this incident and our faith for several more hours. I was not immediately cured and feeling wonderful again. But I realized I was leaving the horrible depression. I didn't suddenly have all the answers, yet, I felt better. I had been reminded of God's presence.

A NEW FAMILY

When I had had physical problems, I saw a doctor and he enabled me to walk. Now, seeing a counselor had enabled me, emotionally, to walk again. Even to dance.

A friend asked me to go to a birthday party. (This is the friend who always said, "I love hanging out with Ward because if one of us gets hit by lightning, it will be Ward and not me.") For me, the worst thing about parties is dancing. I hate to dance. Yet, to meet someone, it seemed you had to ask them to dance. I usually just stood in the middle of the floor, talking to everyone, while people danced around me—not something that most women appreciated. For the most part, tonight was no different.

But, later in the evening, I had noticed, and then begun visiting with, Donna. We hit it off right away, and I was having one of the greatest evenings ever. Everything was going perfectly until Donna mentioned that she loved to dance.

I thought, "Oh great." Aloud, I muttered, "Would you like to dance?"

She accepted with excitement and we headed to the dance floor. There Donna was right at home and quite the dancer. I, on the other hand, pretended to dance for a moment and then began visiting with everyone.

That's when it happened. Donna clearly recognized I didn't like to dance, and didn't seem to mind me just standing there next to her. She danced, and I talked with her and everyone around us. The rest of the evening flew by.

When people began to leave, she invited me over to her house to continue our conversation. I was happy to go (for one thing, no more dancing). I was following her home, but got lost in traffic. While trying to find which way she had gone, I said a prayer, made several turns, and, thankfully, ended up in the right place. There we visited until the early morning hours.

Over the next months, we began to spend a lot of time together, enjoying each other's company—and learning how opposite we were. As already noted, Donna loved to dance, and I did not. Donna loved healthy food, and I loved fast food. She loved to shop; I didn't. Donna loved picnics; I hated eating outside.

I loved sports, and Donna didn't know the difference between a touchdown and a home run. In fact, once, at a baseball game, when the coach took out the opposing team's pitcher because our team was scoring so many runs, she almost started crying. When I asked what was wrong, she said, "That poor pitcher will get his feelings hurt."

We were so different, yet loved being together.

Donna was a single mom with two children, one-year-old Pam and Charlie, aged two. Her tough life, especially over the previous few years, did give us something in common. We had both overcome many odds to get where we were. Thus, although we were very different, we were also very much the same.

For example, Donna was an only child, whose parents had divorced when she was thirteen. Although there had been some difficult times, both parents loved her very much. I had a large extended family that constantly laughed, teased, and most important, loved one another. In fact, our family reunions consisted of more than one hundred people hailing from Connecticut to California. The fact that we both came from loving families seemed to be the most important thing.

During our first Christmas together, I dressed up as Santa for her kids and others in her neighborhood. With a borrowed suit, and some small toys and candy, I spent more than an hour getting ready. I was so excited, and my costume was perfect. I looked just like the real, jolly old elf.

"These kids are going to be so happy," I thought, as I walked next door where about ten children under the age of six were waiting for a surprise arrival.

"Ho, ho, ho," I said as I entered the neighbor's front door, carrying my bag full of goodies. I continued calling, "Ho, ho, ho."

The kids screamed with joy and were as happy as I'd ever seen them. I was so proud of myself, making them all so proud to see Santa in person. "Ho, ho, ho, Merry Christmas!"

Then, suddenly, each and every child started cheering, "Yea, Ward! That's a great costume. Yea, Ward!"

I had disguised my voice. How could they have known it was me? My hobble must have given me away. Laughing together, we all had a fun evening.

KIDS

I had thought I would never get too serious about anyone with children, but now I found that, as I began falling in love with Donna, I was also falling in love with her kids. Charlie was very smart and full of energy. Pam was always smiling and seemed so content. We had so much fun together.

Donna, Charlie, and Pam had accepted me since the day we met. Or was I finally accepting myself?

I finished my associate's degree and enrolled in broadcasting school, returning again to the field that had long interested me. I enjoyed the course immensely, concentrating on TV, though I remember a few people telling me I should focus on radio. I always laughed, and asked if they felt I wasn't good-looking enough for television. I graduated with honors, received three other awards, and was offered a radio station internship that would probably turn into a job.

At the same time, however, an old friend called, and I was offered a job with emotionally disturbed children. I loved working with the physically disabled and thought working with the emotionally disturbed would be the same. I debated for a few days, then decided to take the job with the kids.

With much excitement, I began working at a home for young people aged twelve through fifteen. For the first few months I was told how well I was doing. I loved the job and felt I was making a difference. Management liked my work so much that they wanted me to transfer to a more difficult place, where the kids were harder to help and more violent. The violent part did make me nervous. I voiced my concerns, and management understood, agreeing I would be there only for a short while.

I'd been in the new facility for just a few weeks when one of the residents got angry at me for no apparent reason. I told him to quit messing around and go to bed. When I turned to leave, he kicked me very hard in the back, then yelled to the other kids, who began running through the house, throwing things. One grabbed a fire extinguisher, spraying it everywhere. My friend, Dave, the other employee on duty, helped restrain one child, as I tried to restrain another. Someone threw a big lamp at me; fortunately, I was able to somewhat block the impact.

I was kicked, punched, pushed, and spit on, during this several-minute scuffle, and, thank God, wasn't hurt even worse. We had been trained in how to restrain the children when there was a problem, and, although it was difficult, I did the best I could. Dave was about three times my size, and, if he had not been there, I don't know what would have happened. He did a great job in settling the others down.

I was always more vulnerable because of my underlying physical problems and now I had to undergo another surgery, so doctors could put a piece of my hipbone into my neck.

I was saddened and upset that this had happened, and another surgery was definitely not high on my list, but I knew what these young people had done was not personal. I also realized I had matured because I really wasn't ever angry at them. I understood I truly had to forgive these kids.

It was always easy to love my mom and dad, and others who loved me. But it is hard to forgive and not hold anger toward people who have hurt us. When the Pope forgave and even visited the man who tried to assassinate him, I saw in that the love of God. In fact, I cannot think of a better example in today's society of forgiveness and living one's faith.

I had been taught that, no matter how bad my life seems, I must always try and look for the good in everything. Or, as a friend once told me, "to look for God in everything." Now I knew anger and resentment would not do me any good, and wouldn't affect the people who hurt me anyway.

While I was still in the hospital following the surgery, Donna came to visit dressed as a clown. Donna was not someone I had imagined would dress up, so I laughed even more and recognized what a very nice gesture it was on her part.

There have been many people in my life I consider a blessing and a gift from God, but only a few who were totally accepting, loving, caring, and understanding, and who did not pity or feel sorry for me. Donna was one, and, as we continued to talk and get to know each other, I realized more and more how much I cared for her and for her children.

A BIG STEP

Recovery took months filled with numerous headaches and plenty of therapy. One evening during that time—and while I was sporting a very fashionable neck brace—Donna and I sat in a church parking lot discussing our relationship and how happy both of us were. God had provided; God had brought into my life the most wonderful person, and, as always, His timing was perfect. Now it was time for me to act. I reached into my pocket, pulled out a little box with a ring inside, and asked Donna to marry me.

"Yes," she said. Need I say, this was one of the happiest days of my life?

We did not want a big wedding, so I asked my younger brother, Chris, and his wife, Carrie, to go with us to Reno, Nevada, for the big day. Years before Chris and Carrie had even started dating, she had seen me on television after my bicycle ride across the United States. When they met, Carrie asked Chris if I was his brother. I am sure he proudly said yes. I now remind them jokingly that my notoriety was the main reason Carrie agreed to date Chris.

Chris drove the four of us, plus Pam and Charlie, to Reno early one evening. Still in my neck brace, I know I was not looking my best when we pulled into town. Almost immediately, while we were at a stoplight, a kid, driving his parents' car without a license, came around the corner too fast and crashed into us.

"I hope this isn't a sign," I said as I got out of the car unscathed. The kid did look completely shocked to see me already in a neck brace.

The fender-bender hurt no one, but Donna then reminded us that her original wedding dress had been destroyed when the store in which it had been on layaway burned down. We went ahead with the ceremony, knowing both of our lives had had a lot of drama. Why should our wedding be any different?

As we said our *I do*s, Chris was busy snapping pictures of this special occasion. The chapel ceremony took about five minutes, and the kids thought even that was a little long. When it was over, we headed to the nearest casino to eat and share wonderful memories.

As we walked in, I dropped a dollar in a slot machine and won a $100 jackpot—enough to pay for dinner and our extravagant wedding!

We were all happily enjoying our meal and having a great time when Chris suddenly looked downcast. "What's wrong?" I asked.

Chris muttered, "Well, I am sorry, but I forgot to put film in the camera."

Chris had been in charge of two things—driving us to Reno safely and taking pictures. What a day. We were in a wreck, and we never needed a wedding photo album.

Still the memories are wonderful, including those of a reception held soon after our return, when my mother and father invited more than 100 people to a beautiful restaurant for dinner. We had a great celebration with our closest family and friends.

HUSBAND, FATHER, SON-IN-LAW

Marrying Donna also meant taking on the responsibility of raising her two children and that was not a problem, as I had grown to love them as much as Donna.

The week after the wedding, I began the process of legally adopting Pam and Charlie. When the day arrived for our visit to the judge, I—a huge Notre Dame fan—was quite shocked to see on the wall of his chambers his diploma from USC. Thank goodness, he did not hold that against me. After asking the kids a couple of questions (that they answered very well), we were on our way as a new family. We went out to lunch, played miniature golf, and a lot of video games. We called this wonderful day, "Foley Family Fun Day," and the kids went from calling me Ward, to calling me Dad.

Soon after we were married, Donna had a call from her father, Richard, in Nevada. Richard had decided he would move in with us. He said he could help us with the kids and cooking and other needs we might have. Of course, it wouldn't be because he was seventy-five years old and might need our help. We were happy to have not only him live with us, but also his best friends, dog Muffin and cat Sam (six toes on each paw).

In a year's time, I had gone from being single to being married with two kids, and housing a father-in-law, dog, and six-toed cat.

Charlie attended kindergarten. At our first parent-teacher conference, the teacher said he talked all the time, sometimes even when he wasn't supposed to, but was a very good child. The teacher did have one concern. She said, "Charlie always knocks another boy's hat off, and thinks it is funny."

When we arrived home, I told Donna I had a great idea for how to teach Charlie a lesson. I called him over and knocked off his hat. He looked a little startled as he put his hat back on. I again knocked it off. Charlie immediately started laughing and said, "Hey, Dad, that's funny; I do that to this kid at school every day!"

Pam, just a toddler, went to what we called "Ward School." This school consisted mostly of playing lots of games and watching *The Price is Right* and *The Golden Girls*. At times, however, Ward School could be a little dangerous.

One afternoon, when Pam was standing on the couch, I told her to be careful because there were sharks where the carpet was. Before I knew it, she was jumping to the coffee table, where she slipped and cut open her lip. While tending to her bleeding wound, I asked her why she had jumped. Pam said she didn't want to get bitten by the sharks. I felt horrible; fortunately, no stitches were needed.

The kids truly were great kids, and I was so proud to be their father.

When T-Ball (baseball for little kids) started, I volunteered to coach Charlie's team. This was not meant to be competitive; I don't think we were even supposed to keep score. (Although, being a little competitive, I did.)

Coaching Charlie and the other kids was a lot of fun except that one of the parents seemed to have a problem with me. He would question everything I did and always had a smart-aleck remark. I wasn't sure if his problem was with all disabled people or just me.

As the season progressed, his remarks became more belligerent. Before the start of one game, I was leaning against our dugout watching another coach warming up our team when this man approached me.

I thought, "Here we go again." Yet, I was ready for anything when this man said, "Hey Ward, when you were a kid, with your hands like that, how did you ever play with yourself?"

Disgusted but not surprised, I immediately responded with, "Oh, I just had the neighbor lady do it."

When I was a child, I'd thought people would grow up and this kind of thing would no longer happen, but had learned that there were rude and ignorant people everywhere, of every age and both sexes. I was not going to let this one hurt me. If I got mad, or let what he said bother me, he won.

Even friends and loved ones can do or say things that hurt us. One afternoon, Richard was waiting for me to get home and take him to a doctor's appointment. When I walked in the door, late, he was angrier than I had ever seen him. He immediately started yelling at me, not a common occurrence.

Then he said, "You're just a f---ing cripple." I was a little shocked at first, but then laughed, which probably wasn't the best thing to do.

"Oh, you can do better than that. I've been called a cripple my whole life." I asked, "Would you like to know why I am late?" Without giving him time to answer, I said, "I had to go pick up your daughter from work and take her to the emergency room. Donna wasn't feeling well."

He suddenly became quiet and I could tell he felt horrible. I even felt bad for him, though he had needed to understand what had happened. Not many words were spoken on the way to and from his appointment. When we arrived home, Richard handed me a five-dollar bill, thanked me for the ride, and told me to use the money for gas. Five dollars was a lot for him, and, though I was still a little hurt, I understood that this was his apology.

These incidents—the parent making rude comments and Richard getting upset with me—were offensive, and my writing about them may offend some people, too. But these and others like them have offended me throughout my life.

My reaction to them, however, helped me see that I was maturing, and beginning truly to accept and like who I was. Others could no longer break the confidence I had in myself. I could love myself when somebody loved me, and I could love myself when others were angry at or even hated me. I was no longer reacting with anger or frustration, but only sadness at others' ignorance and their inability to understand and accept that we all are different.

In other words, I was beginning to see the advantages of my struggles in life.

LIGHTS OUT

My first encounter with Glenn was not the greatest of first meetings. On a hot summer day, I stopped by the home of my friend, Lynne, for a visit. I asked her to get a heavy box out of my car, and Glenn, whom I had just met, got angry: "Do not ask a lady to lift something so heavy."

At the time, of course, he didn't realize I was unable to do certain things, but Glenn also had an attitude problem. I often described him as a typical referee—stubborn, always right, and with a chip on his shoulder. We did, however, become good friends, and, in fact, I was honored to be the best man at their wedding.

A few years into a wonderful marriage to Lynne, Glenn was suddenly stricken with cancer. He fought the disease with numerous trips to doctors, agonizing chemotherapy treatments, and experimental procedures, but nothing slowed the growth of his brain tumor.

A few weeks before his death, we had a fantastic visit. Glenn had become the most peaceful person I had ever met. He was content. He understood the importance of all the little things in life. He had learned to appreciate flowers, birds, family and friends, love. I was in awe. Glenn was relaxed and ready to die. The change in him, from before cancer to after, was night and day. He was filled with God's love. I couldn't believe what I was seeing. It was as if God had given him all the answers.

Glenn told me how he felt so blessed. He was dying and yet happy, the happiest I had ever seen him, not wanting or needing anything. He had an incredible peace, and I wanted that peace more than anything.

Several weeks after Glenn's death, Lynne and I were talking on the phone late one evening, sharing stories about him and the beauty he had brought to both of our lives. It was then she told me about something that had occurred within the last days of Glenn's life. As Lynne had sat beside her husband's bed, he had told her, "Lynne, every time a light bulb burns out, I want you to think of me."

I then asked her if any light bulbs had burned out.

Lynne said, "All the time, and I am getting tired of changing them." I laughed and we finished our conversation.

"That's a neat story," I thought, as I hung up the phone and headed to bed. I flipped the light switch on and began walking down the hallway. A few steps later, the light bulb went out. Whoa!

That incident was only the first of many times that lights burned out in my presence. Invariably, it happened when I had been thinking about Glenn. Like the time I thought about him as I entered the bathroom. Boom! Lights out! I thought, "This is no coincidence!" A few minutes later, while I was still in awe, the phone rang. It was Lynne!

Years later Lynne told me that, while driving home one evening, she noticed several streetlights going out along her route. As always, she thought of her late husband and wondered what this message might mean. The very next evening it happened again, but with a different set of lights. Thinking of Glenn and many other of God's gifts had brought her peace, so she wasn't uptight or nervous. Still she wondered what this message might mean.

The following morning, Lynne's mother passed away, a sad event made much easier for Lynne to accept because the lights had let her know her mother would be fine.

These stories of Lynne and Glenn and lights going out have long been special to me, so I shared them with my brother Craig and his wife, Anna, when her mother died. They kindly listened to my stories, but didn't say much. It wasn't until I left their house that the message became real to them. After saying goodbye, I stepped outside, Anna turned the porch light on for me, and, bingo, out went the light.

While writing these stories, three light bulbs in my house have gone out—one in the kitchen, one in the dining room, one in the living room. I'd better wrap up this chapter so I won't have to buy any more bulbs!

Are these signs or something that just happened? What did they mean? Were God and Glenn telling Lynne something? I may never know the answers to these questions, but I do know these "lights out" brought comfort to Lynne and to others.

I also knew Lynne had never had much religion or understanding of God in her life. After the deaths of her husband and mother, the experience of the lights going out seemed to trigger a desire in Lynne to begin searching for a belief in, or understanding of, God.

Personally, I think the lights going out is kind of neat. Some years later, all the power in our small town went off around midnight. My cousin Annie, a little nervous, called, wondering what had happened. "I'm not sure, although someone very close to us may have just died," I joked.

Whenever a bulb burns out, I am reminded of my old friend Glenn, and I am thankful to God for showing me the peace I saw in him before his death.

A GROWING PRESENCE

The lady in white who helped after my car accident had been an obvious sign of God's presence. Now, however, I was beginning to feel that presence more often in my daily life.

I had been raised Roman Catholic, went to church nearly every Sunday, and believed in Jesus. I prayed and even talked to God on occasion, especially when I needed help. Yet, most of my life, I had just been going through the motions, scattering prayers here and there, counting on God for love and support only at certain times. During surgeries, I asked for assistance and He eased the pain. When I was teased and laughed at, I asked for comfort and He befriended me. When I became depressed, I asked for help and He guided me. Whatever the problem, He was with me, teaching me.

During "problems" were the times I most turned to Him. I was always thankful for the wonderful things in my life and, especially, the love of all my family and friends. But, like many of us, I had mostly called on God when things were hard. Now I found myself praying in both bad times and good.

God had revealed Himself to me in a different way through Glenn's death. I had seen in Glenn the love of God we should all be searching for. I was now seeing clearly where I had been and where I wanted to be. I immediately began reading the Bible and praying for that peace. I wanted the peace I had seen in Glenn.

And I wanted that peace without having to die to get it.

ANOTHER GOODBYE

Early one morning, Donna and the kids and I went to visit her mother, Jean. Pam and Charlie called this grandma, "Bay Area Grandma," as she lived in the San Francisco Bay area. We spent the whole day shopping and eating, and, as always, Jean enjoyed spoiling her grandkids and us as well.

Jean and I had become very close over the years. She had always been nice to me, but, when Donna and I were dating, Jean voiced her concerns to Donna about marrying me.

At the time I was very defensive, feeling this was an attack on my accomplishments and independence, and knowing that something could happen to Donna, or anyone for that matter, and they could find themselves in the same predicament.

Jean had pointed out to Donna the difficulties that could arise with my condition and asked her to consider carefully if she'd be able to deal with possibly having to take care of me. Then there were the daily activities Donna would have to take care of, because I was unable. Such tasks as mowing the lawn or trimming the trees were simply too hard for me physically. These were real concerns and, looking back, I see not only my growth since then, but realize this was not an attack on me. These were just questions any caring parents should have for their children.

While we were away visiting Jean, Richard was alone at home, and in trouble.

He had walked out into the backyard, fallen, and couldn't get up. He did manage to crawl to his bedroom, where he lay for several hours until we arrived home that evening. I immediately took him to the emergency room where we waited another six hours for a doctor to see him. He had numerous bruises and had torn the rotator cuff in one shoulder.

Many times I had taken Richard to the doctor's office or grocery store, and I had worried that he would fall. I knew my instinct would be to try to catch him, even though I also knew very well I would hurt myself because I was much weaker and weighed much less. I had told Richard that, if he fell, I would not be able to catch him. I would have to let him fall, and the thought made me feel so helpless. Richard understood, however, and didn't even expect me to try.

Because of this fall, and some other incidents, we were no longer able to take care of him. At his doctor's suggestion, we decided Richard would have to live in an assisted care facility.

The devastating day came when I took him to his new home. He was as polite and as nice as could be, and it turned out to be a great fit for Richard. Still, as I drove away with tears rolling down my face, a great sadness came over me. Even though I knew we were doing the right thing, the only thing, this was still very difficult.

Richard enjoyed the facility as best as he could. He was able to take his dog, Muffin, which made him very happy. He adapted well and even complained about the ladies trying to pick him up. "These women just won't leave me alone," he would say.

Donna and I tried to visit Richard several times a week, and he always had a list of things he needed. I think he had this list of errands to ensure we would be back, and I was happy to oblige.

About a year later, Richard was diagnosed with cancer throughout his body. He didn't have much time left, and we were told hospice could help. In my first experience with hospice, we met a nurse and social worker at the hospital, and they told us everything we needed to know.

Richard had always been a very proud man. Even in his late seventies, he worked out with weights, and, unfortunately, lay out in our backyard in his Speedo to get a tan. He was so proud of his physique; he'd worked out with Jack LaLanne in his younger years. (I can see now what they mean when they say a daughter marries a person a lot like her father. I was rather skinny and weighed in at about 120 pounds.)

While Richard lay in his hospital bed preparing to die, at a suggestion from hospice, we put pictures of him in his younger years all over the walls. Many times, nurses and other staff members would admire him because of the pictures. Though he looked close to death, the pictures helped bring him alive to others.

Late one Saturday morning, Richard's brother and niece came for a visit. Within an hour, Richard went into a coma. Later that afternoon, the doctors told us he could die at any minute.

Donna wanted someone to be with her dad at all times. An only child, she did not want her dad to die alone. So she and I took turns sitting at his bedside, hour after hour.

Day after day. We had been told he was going to die and he just didn't. Part of me thought there was a reason, but I couldn't figure it out.

Late in the evening, three days later, I was sitting alone with Richard in his comatose state. It hurt to watch and listen to him struggle to breathe. I began praying, "Please Lord, help Richard, and give me a sign letting me know what to do."

Richard's roommate had not said a word for a week. Suddenly, about midnight, I heard him yell, "What the hell are you doing here?"

A little startled, I said, "I am here helping Richard."

"Go home. You're not doing him any good."

Not another word was said. I heard only Richard's breathing and the beeping sounds of monitors. I began reflecting on what had just happened. Was God trying to tell me something?

Richard had always been a private person. Even when he lived with us, he loved being alone in his room. He loved long walks by himself. He had been predicted to die days ago, but he kept struggling to breathe. Maybe I should leave. Maybe he just wants to die alone, without Donna or me here. I sat for a few minutes praying and then knew it was time for me to go.

I told Richard how much we all loved him and thanked him for all his support. I told Richard that he could move on, and then said good-bye—one of the hardest goodbyes I have ever had to say.

When I got home, I told Donna what had happened, and she understood why I left. Within two hours, the hospital called and said Richard had passed away. It all made sense. He had died the way he lived, privately and independently.

Had I heard from God, and had God directed me?

The next day, the most wonderful feeling came over me. Although I felt great sadness at Richard's death, I also had a sense that what I had done for Richard over the years was one of the best things I had ever done.

My whole life I had tried doing wonderful things. I had bicycled across the United States and Canada. I had written a book. I had spoken at schools and churches. Yet, that had not been as important as the love I had shown toward Richard. No matter how upset he made me at times, I had always tried to do for Richard what I had thought God would want.

Now God had given me a beautiful feeling of love, of peace, and of more than I can even begin to put into words. It was that same peace I had seen in Glenn before he died, that peace I had prayed for. I truly felt God's love, as if He were giving me a taste or a sample, allowing me to experience just a bit of that true peace.

Now I wanted even more. I wanted that peace in my life every day. My prayers intensified, as I knew this journey to peace was just beginning.

MOVING ON

Donna and I put our house up for sale, for a number of reasons, but mostly because we thought we could provide a better life for our kids in Norton, Kansas, a small town where many members of my extended family already lived.

For me, the biggest drawback of a move would be losing my doctors, especially Dr. Boutin. He had helped so much with all my physical problems, and his compassion and love for me were always evident. I would miss him greatly. I would also miss other family and friends, but I was ready to move.

Donna had worked for the City of Sacramento for several years, had received numerous promotions, and loved her job. She also loved the malls and spending time shopping with her best friend, Dana. She would miss her Mom a great deal, too. Despite all that, she was also ready to move.

The only problem was that our house would not sell. In fact, it was shown only five times in more than three years. So, though Donna and I were prepared, it was obvious God wasn't quite ready for us to go yet.

We were hoping to move before the kids started junior high. Things were happening in our neighborhood, and we felt God was leading us to the Midwest. Once the doorbell rang at two in the morning. The police were asking if they could go into our backyard and look for a criminal. Nice of them to ask, but by the time I managed to reach the door, the criminal was probably gone.

On another occasion, we heard a gunshot outside our bedroom late in the evening. Donna got the kids and lay in the hallway, while I called 911. The dispatcher told me, if I heard the gun again, to give them a call. Wondering how I would do that with a bullet lodged in me, I said, "Okay."

After these and a few other incidents, I told Donna if someone broke into our house, we needed a plan. Since I was "Mr. Mom" in our household, I suggested, "You fend off the attackers, and I'll run out the back door for help."

My nerves were telling me a small town would be better. Norton, Kansas, was a place where you could still sleep with the windows open and leave your keys in the car. But we couldn't go until we sold our house. As the years passed, I couldn't understand why our house wasn't selling. We tried numerous real estate agents with no luck. Although I was frustrated, I knew, deep down, that when it was the right time—God's time—our house would sell.

My parents suddenly decided they would move to Norton, too, and put their house up for sale. Three months after Richard's death, our house and theirs sold on the same day. It was "God's time," and we could now move with His blessing. The kids had not yet reached junior high; Charlie was in sixth grade and Pam, fifth. Another one of God's little blessings was that we could share a moving van with my parents and keep our costs way down.

With our van packed, the four of us and our dog, Moo, met my parents at my Aunt Nadyne's apartment. We told Nadyne and my cousin Annie goodbye, and that we hoped they would think about moving to Norton someday. "Never," said Nadyne. Within a year, their family was living in Norton, too.

A NEW HOME...

Three days later we arrived in Norton, Kansas. Home of the International BB Gun Champions, and of the best pheasant hunters and best farmers in the world. Home not of garage sales, but of auctions. Home of many wonderful things, none of which I knew anything about. Except that this was also the home of my ninety-three-year-old grandma, my Uncle Jack and Aunt Esther, my Aunt Mary Kay and Uncle Jack, two of my brothers and their families, and the new home of my parents. I came to find out that most people in this town of about three thousand were somehow related. (That's good and bad.)

Having my two older brothers and their families in the same town was one of the best parts of moving to Norton. Kirk and his wife, Janie, have four girls, Megan, Maggie, Allison, and Kayla. I loved hanging out with my nieces. When Megan was young, I would always take her out and show her off. That ended when Megan was in junior high and fixed her hair so the bangs stood up three feet high.

Craig and Anna have two children, Erin Marie and Jared. When I was in my late teens, Craig and Anna had written a beautiful letter nominating me for the "Most Inspirational Handicapped Person" in northern California. I didn't come in first, but I was a runner-up. I always tell them, had their writing skills been better, I would have won.

A drawback of living in Norton was being so far from Chris, the youngest of us four boys, who still lived in California. Chris and Carrie have four children, Ryan, Davis, Matthew, and Tana. Ryan was named after Chris's favorite pitcher, Nolan Ryan; Davis was named after the city in California where they first met; Tana was the closest thing to Joe Montana Carrie would approve; and I was honored when they named Matthew after me, Matthew Ward Foley.

I was impressed that they named one child after a city, and the other three after famous people.

... NEW EXPERIENCES ...

Not just my relatives, but all the people of Norton were very friendly and welcomed our family to their town.

In fact, the first thing I noticed in Norton was everyone waving hello and goodbye as they passed me in the car—and not with their middle fingers, as was the custom in California.

That wasn't the only difference I noticed between driving on the highways of Kansas instead of California. In the city, I hadn't had to be aware of so many animals (in a literal sense). Coming back early one evening by myself from a sporting event, I was four miles from home when I noticed something up ahead. I put my foot on the brake and gradually slowed.

I suddenly realized there were three deer in the middle of the road. "Oh Jesus, help me," I yelled, and pressed the brake even harder.

A good friend had hit a couple of deer in a year's time, and been hurt by the air bag, and he was a lot bigger than I was. So I had a great fear of air bags, so much so that a state trooper friend, Doug Griffiths, had given me a bulletproof vest to wear while driving, to help protect my chest. Now, however, the vest was underneath my seat and not going to be much help.

Having been told never to swerve, I gripped the steering wheel tightly and headed directly into all three deer. I could see them looking at me as I came within ten feet. I closed my eyes, knowing I was about to crash, fearing the pain of the discharging air bag.

"Jesus, help me," I prayed again.

When nothing had happened a second later, I opened my eyes and the deer were gone. I couldn't believe I had driven right through them. The deer must have been praying, too.

In Norton I can run several errands and be home within ten minutes. A traffic jam consists of being behind four cars at the only stoplight in town. I've heard gunshots, but, here, they're made by hunters. Friends say if you don't like the weather, just wait twenty minutes.

One of my most enjoyable days here was the grand opening of Norton's Taco Bell. I love the food, and it brings back many happy memories of my first job. Dad used to tell me there are no free lunches in life, and, yet, nearly every time I eat at Pizza Hut/Taco Bell, Dan or Jeannie gives me a free lunch. (The last sentence was sponsored, and written in hopes of continuing my free lunches.)

As we had hoped, Norton seemed to be a great place to raise kids. Both Pam and Charlie adapted well and made new friends quickly, and the school system is wonderful. The band teacher, Mr. Will, even marches with the kids during the halftime of football games and, in my opinion, is one of the best teachers we have. I may be a little biased, however, because he is also my neighbor and has provided a helping hand for our family whenever needed.

... AND A NEW TEAM

Baseball has been my favorite sport since my days playing Little League. So it was not surprising that I coached Charlie throughout his Little League years. Countless hours were spent playing catch, and with me hitting ground balls to him. Fortunately, I had a great friend Ken whose son Robert was the same age as Charlie. We coached together, and, when I got tired, I could rest and he would work with the kids.

Baseball was a year-round sport in California. What a shock when we moved to Kansas, where baseball was played for about a month, and like a picnic game. Baseball just wasn't a priority in the small town of Norton, Kansas—until I arrived. I was going to do my best to bring back baseball. After all, years ago, Norton had been a huge baseball town, hosting many greats as they passed through on their way to the majors. Clete Boyer, Elden Auker, and Billy Martin all had played here, and so did my Uncle Jack Ward who, though he never made it to the majors, will always be a big leaguer in my eyes.

My first goal was to put together a twelve-and-under traveling team. My cousin Dave Ward and my brother Craig helped in this endeavor.

We had our first practice, and everyone was excited, especially me. The kids were lacking most fundamentals and knowledge of the game, but the best way to learn was by playing a lot. I made hundreds of phone calls to set up a schedule. Not knowing the area made it difficult. But I was determined to get these kids at least thirty games that year.

One of our first stops was a small Nebraska town, Naponee. I was a little nervous when I learned most of the parents had never heard of it. When we pulled into Naponee, we found about four buildings and their little "field of dreams," covered with weeds, rocks, and stickers, and with a huge trash burn still smoking (and smelling) in center field. Hit the ball into the fire, and it was pretty sure to be a home run.

Once we put the bases down, we could tell where to run. A little old fence became a backstop. There was barely a fence in front of our dugout, with its team bench that may have held six players. The fans were expected to sit on cement "bleachers" on a day that reached over 100 degrees. The snack bar was a Pepsi machine a block away, near an abandoned building.

And I had thought Norton was small.

The other team arrived, not on a bus, not even in cars, but on tractors, and they weren't wearing uniforms, but cowboy apparel, such as boots and cowboy hats. Some wore shorts. These kids had truly just left their farms to come and play a little baseball, but they and their fans were excited to play our well-dressed team, sporting new uniforms from Jack Ward's Sporting Goods.

The Naponee kids didn't care if they won or lost, they were just happy to get away from work for awhile. But all my parents and coaches looked at me as if I had been crazy to set up this game. We won the doubleheader easily, but the lessons and memories were countless.

As with any team, ours was full of different but wonderful personalities. Dave's son Matt was on the team, and, like his Grandpa Jack, he was a catcher. Though he was a year younger than most of the rest of the kids, no one would have guessed. Matt was as proud of others' success as he was his own. Whether he played every inning or just batted once, he was always happy.

One day during practice, I told him that he was named after the famous Me—Matthew Ward Foley.

With his wonderful grin and joyous laugh, he said, "Oh, good one. You're funny."

"Really," I said. I then took out my driver's license and showed him my full name.

"Whoa," Matt said, and then yelled to his dad, "Hey, did you know I was named after Ward?" Matt's attitude and personality truly made him a coach's dream player.

Later that summer, we played a team from Manhattan, Kansas, who just knew they were going to destroy us, and they did—the first couple of innings. We were the small-town team now.

Then Joel Griffiths came to bat. Joel was the team leader, not necessarily because of his baseball ability, but because of his comedic personality, jolly physique, and carefree, fun-loving attitude. I wanted to pinch-hit for Joel because he had a low batting average, and we needed some hits. But this was an age for learning, and winning wasn't as important as these kids playing together. Joel managed to draw a walk and get on first base. The kids in our dugout went nuts; I was somewhat surprised myself, and happy I had let him bat.

The first pitch to the next batter was a ball and there went Joel stealing second base. "What is he doing?" I thought. The umpire yelled, "Safe!" Matt, my nephew Jared, and all the kids were screaming, yelling, and chanting, "Jo-el, Jo-el." Our next batter hit his first pitch to the fence for a double, and in came Joel to score a run. Our team went on to beat the big-city team 12–11, and continued improving throughout the year. More important, we made many wonderful memories.

TRAGEDY

The following summer, on the Fourth of July, our celebration was interrupted by Norton's sirens. In a small town, everyone is concerned. Within minutes, we saw the ambulance drive by. Soon we learned there had been a terrible accident involving one of our players, and not just any player—my cousin's son, my namesake, Matt.

Matt and a friend had been playing with their BB guns and a BB had ricocheted off a pole into Matt's head. Now Matt was flown to a larger hospital as doctors did everything possible to save his life.

Later that day, our whole town was dealt a tragic blow. Matt Ward died. He was only twelve.

Death can be a horrible experience, especially when it involves a child. Matt had been so full of life and accepting of everyone. He always had a smile and a caring heart. I will never forget how happy his excitement made me feel. He had made anyone he was with feel important.

Why would a loving God do this, or allow it to happen? Why would He take somebody so young, someone who brought happiness to so many? These and many questions run through our minds in such situations, and there are no easy answers. In fact, there are no answers at all. This is about faith. Trusting in God is all we have. I think Matt's mother, Donna, said it best: "I believe fifteen seconds after I die, I will have an *aha* moment, and will understand it all."

I heard someone say that it is not a life cut short, it's a completed soul. Matt's soul was definitely completed. That sparkle in his eye and zest for life will always be remembered. Matt's motto—"Just Do Your Best"—lives on, and was adopted as their own by his classmates when they graduated from Norton High School in 2005.

THAT CHAMPIONSHIP SEASON

No matter how devastating our tragedies, we must still live our lives, and Matt, more than anyone, would have wanted us to move on. We kept on playing more than thirty games a year, and the team continued to improve and have more success. When most of the kids were fifteen, we set our sights high—on the state title. Since the state championship had begun more than fifty years before, Norton had finished second, but had never won.

This season, I had been unable to coach. I had lost a lot of weight, and being below 115 pounds was making me sick. I continued to help, however, by organizing the team, setting up the schedule, and trying to keep all the parents happy. (Believe me, that could be the hardest job.)

We had a great season and reached the state championship game with a 30–4 record. The only problem was that we now had to play again the team that had given us all four losses. Hays, Kansas, is a town about five times the size of ours, and they pulled up to the field in a bus used by the Hays Larks, a semipro team.

We jumped out to an early 2–1 lead. Then their biggest player hit a three-run homer, and we fell behind. Still, our kids never gave up and continued to play hard, and in the last inning we had key hits, putting us ahead 8–7.

With two outs in the bottom of the last inning, Hays had runners on second and third bases. Tyler Rutherford pitched and their batter hit a slow grounder down the third base line. My Charlie, playing third, picked up the ball and threw it in the dirt to first. The first baseman, Josh Green, scooped it up, held the ball tightly, and the umpire yelled, "You're out!"

We were State Champions! The players and the Norton crowd went nuts, jumping up and down, hugging everyone within reach, as if we had won the World Series. For these kids, that's exactly what we'd done.

The players' names were each announced as they were given their trophies. Then it was revealed that our team had also won the sportsmanship award.

We had overcome humble beginnings and tragedy to reach this point of triumph. Now we were the pride of Norton, a town that had once been only our family's dream.

GROWTH THROUGH CHALLENGE

The church I was attending called with a request. Because of a lack of volunteers, they'd been unable to find a teacher for a confirmation class of about thirty kids. They asked my cousin Annie (one of the most spiritual people I know) and me if we would teach the class together, a two-year commitment.

Although I'd been raised Roman Catholic, I'd attended a variety of Christian churches throughout my adult life. And though Donna had been raised in a Lutheran church, we had raised our children as Catholics. My mom always said, "Once a Catholic, always a Catholic," and this seemed to hold true for me. No matter how many other churches I attended, I always appreciated the Catholic mass the most.

I felt teaching confirmation and about the Holy Spirit not only would help me learn, but also was another way of helping others. I accepted.

The class went very well, until it was time for the confirmands to pick their sponsors. My nephew Jared chose me, a great compliment; I was very proud. That is, until a leader in the church told me I could not be Jared's sponsor.

"Why not?"

"Because you are in bad standing with the church."

"What did I do?"

"When you were married, you weren't married in a Catholic church," she said.

I thought, "But I was married in Reno, and I gambled, winning enough money to pay for our wedding. Isn't that being a good Catholic?" Aloud, however, I responded, "I told Father the reason why I wasn't married in the church when we moved here, and he knew the whole situation. It didn't seem to be a problem."

"Well, I am sorry," she said. "But that's the policy."

I was completely stunned. I could teach thirty kids for two years the importance of the Holy Spirit and confirmation, yet I could not walk down the aisle as a sponsor during the ceremony. This made no sense.

Apparently, I was good enough to teach because no one else would. I was not worthy to be a sponsor because enough others could.

I was saddened by what felt like a personal attack, and I also had many questions. How many people were attending church and taking communion, while cheating on their spouses? How many people were kneeling and praying while thinking evil thoughts about people across the aisle? I had seen many churchgoers judge and condemn others, gossip, attend church for all the wrong reasons. How many people in church used God's name in vain? How many people lived their lives with God only one hour a week?

I knew, however, this was not about anyone else. This was about me.

Church leaders wonder why people quit attending. Sometimes, sadly, it is when people of "religion" chase others away, and this is not just true in my local Roman Catholic church, but everywhere and in every kind of church. A worship service should be a celebration, and a place to share and to grow in our relationships with God. Instead, too often, we bring the hatred, judgment, and politics of life into what is meant to be a place of worship.

Had I said nothing about not being married in the church, no one would have known. Honesty *is* the best policy, and yet, this happened.

My first thought was that I should quit teaching the class, an idea I quickly dismissed because it would hurt the kids, and me. Frustrated, I called Sister Marilyn, a friend I had met through volunteer work in a nearby town. I have always had great respect for priests and nuns, and I certainly did for her. Now I told her about my beliefs and about my disappointments in the Catholic Church. As Sister and I visited, she helped me understand that judgments like this are made by humans and encouraged me to continue trusting in my personal relationship with Jesus.

All churches have rules, and I understand that we need to follow them. But she truly understood where I was and how I was trying to live my life. Sister Marilyn was an answer to many of my prayers. Now I realized that the Church understood my situation, but some parishioners had made their own judgments, judgments that excluded me from being a sponsor.

In my mind, I had a great excuse to quit teaching the class and leave the church. But I didn't. No excuses. And there was no reason to run from God, for He is in control and will make good come of all situations. God led me to Sister Marilyn, who took the time to help me understand my difficulties and disagreements.

I knew the kids would be disappointed if I quit, but, more important, God would be disappointed. Now I felt a sense of peace and saw great growth in myself. And Annie and I finished teaching the class, honored to witness all our students confirmed during their special mass.

LIVING WITH THE CHALLENGES

Just like anywhere else, all was not perfect in Norton.

One morning, I saw men building a ramp to the post office, and noticed they had just finished putting in an automatic door, too.

As I walked into the building, a woman said, "Hey, cripple, let me get the door for you." I couldn't believe what she had said, but I didn't take it personally. I really do not think the woman thought it was wrong to call me a cripple.

Later, I shared this story with Mary Kay, just as I have shared others like it throughout my life. She laughed and said that nothing like that ever happened to her. The following week, however, while in Burger King in a nearby town, Mary Kay was filling her cup with tea when a young lady said to her, "Hey, you're the second cripple we've had in here today." I laughed as she told me the story and was happy this had finally happened to her, too.

No matter where in the world one lives, there are always people who may not understand the differences we all have. So many people have said to me, "Can't kids be so cruel?" True, kids can be cruel, but they are kids, still learning and capable of being taught compassion. Adults who have never fully grown up can also be cruel. Whatever the source, we all need to learn how to deal with others' words and actions.

More than once, another local woman has told me how nice it must be not to have to work. The first two times, I thought she must be kidding. The third time I responded, "It must be nice to not have pain and to be able to sleep through the night."

I responded that way because I wanted her to think and not to be so judgmental. At the same time, I realized that my response showed great growth in my own acceptance. I actually took her words as a compliment, since every time she saw me, I was happy and enjoying life, not whining and complaining.

"Smiling is the easiest thing to do," my mom would say. My lack of many muscles did not affect my smile, and the more I smiled, the better I felt. So did the people around me. We all know people who complain, whine, look for excuses, and believe nothing is ever their fault. Spending time with them drains and exhausts us, and we find ourselves also filled with negativity. On the other hand, when we are around happy, smiling, and positive people, we find ourselves feeling better and looking for the good in life. I was taught by my parents to try to focus always on what I *can* do. If that means just volunteering when I am able, I am still doing the best I can with what I have.

DAY BY DAY

Writing about what I live with physically and emotionally is very difficult because I simply deal with it, and I do not want anyone feeling sorry for me. Even at my worst, I am thankful for what I have. There are so many with even greater problems.

Still, almost every day, my legs and arms, hips, back, or neck hurt. For years, I have had trouble sleeping because the aches and pains make it so hard to get comfortable. In fact, once a doctor suggested I try a mild antidepressant. A few weeks later I reported that I still couldn't sleep, but,

"I sure was a lot happier."

In some ways, having lived with pain my whole life has been a great advantage. I'm mostly able to tune out life's common aches. More difficult to live with is the extreme fatigue. Some days, it takes every ounce of my energy to get a drink of water or even to talk.

On a good day, I think I can do anything, but then there are the days on which I am lucky to get out of bed. When I don't feel well, when the extreme fatigue hits, it is very difficult even to pretend to be happy, or to smile. Compare it to the flu. I ache all over, am nauseated and totally drained. I usually stay home and away from people, or around only a few of my loved ones. Thinking about tomorrow is impossible. My thoughts become skewed, and negative: "I am useless. How can I keep going? How will I feel in a couple of years? Am I giving up?" It is devastating, and, in times like this, I have learned to try not to think. I simply pray more, knowing it will get better, even though I feel the opposite.

In bed, the top sheet causes pain just touching my skin. Thanks to my Uncle Jack Woodyard (Mary Kay's husband), I now have a device that elevates the sheet off my body.

Every morning, getting to the bathroom takes several minutes. My feet are so stiff and weak, I often wonder if I'll make it without falling. One day, only a couple of steps along my journey, I did fall, onto our Labrador, Moo. I felt horrible for Moo, although I was happy I had landed on something soft and hadn't broken anything, on me or Moo. Since this incident, every time I stand up or get out of bed, Moo kindly jumps up quickly and gets several feet away from me. I didn't even have to train her. I am sorry, though, when I have a tough night and get out of bed six or seven times. Moo must not get much sleep either.

Because of the physical challenges I face each day, I have learned to do many things "my own special way." Most of my closest friends don't even know how I struggle to do the simplest of tasks, such as shaving or brushing my teeth—but at least I can.

Shaving does take a lot of energy. I use both hands to hold the razor to my face and gently move my face up, down, and sideways. Brushing my teeth is done with the same technique; I hold the toothbrush and move my head. Some days, when weaker than normal, I have to rest my arms on a dresser in order to get my hands to my face.

Not until I was older did I realize why I choose to eat the foods I do. Of course, one reason is that Mom spoiled us boys by fixing four different dinners at a time. But, mainly, my choices depend on how hard the foods are to eat. The easier it is to hold and lift to my mouth, the more I like the food. That makes most fruits and vegetables not worth the effort. Ice cream, however, doesn't seem to be a problem. Seriously, I love chicken and yet hate eating it, unless it is boneless. A chicken leg is simply too hard to hold to my mouth and eat. I love steak, but, if my wife isn't around to cut it, I'll settle for grilled cheese.

Wearing a shirt with a collar is always a problem. To fix my collar, I bend down with my neck touching the corner of the dresser, and lift up slowly, hoping to catch the collar and turn it under. All these things are just the way I live, and harmless. Well, except for that one time.

In bed, I use my teeth to pull up the covers, or to move my pillow. Half asleep one morning, I grabbed my pillow with my teeth and began moving it—until I heard a horribly loud scream. I immediately woke up to find teeth marks in Donna's arm. What I thought was the pillow, had been Donna's bicep. Thank God we hadn't had an argument the night before.

When Donna went to work that morning at the health department, she asked the nurses if she would need a tetanus shot. When they asked what happened, she explained that her husband had bitten her. I guess not everything I do "my own special way" is always harmless.

FAMILY & FRIENDS

Though Donna might tell you I nearly bit off her arm, she never made me feel bad. She has been a gift in every aspect of my life, wonderful in understanding and accepting what I can and can't do. Not once has she ever made me feel less for being unable to do certain things. Even Pam and Charlie sit quietly, reading, playing, or watching television, if I need to rest.

I have also been blessed with many friends who truly care. For example, Karen called one evening to ask how I felt. I answered her like I do most every time someone asks that question: "Pretty good."

She then said, "No, I mean it. I worked in the yard for several hours today, and now my hands are aching terribly. I can barely use them. I thought this must be how you feel all the time. I called to see how you are really doing." A couple of minutes and a few simple words meant a great deal to me.

However, expecting our family and friends always to understand our difficulties or pain is wrong and sets us up for disappointments. Many times people care, but don't know what to do, how to show it. Many times our loved ones hate seeing us in pain, and, so, try to ignore our struggles. This isn't anyone's fault; it's just the way life is.

None of us can truly understand another's pain, but when others sincerely care, can acknowledge that pain, and listen compassionately with an empathetic heart . . . well, that is a blessing that has enabled me to keep going on days I felt like quitting.

HELPING AND BEING HELPED

By this time, I had come a long way in my life. I wasn't pretending anymore; I had truly accepted myself. Sure, there were going to be things to deal with my whole life, but I had handled the physical and emotional parts. Now I wanted more of the spiritual.

Matt's death had reminded me how precious life is. Having seen the peace in Glenn and experienced a taste of it myself after Richard's death, I began focusing on that most important question: how do I find that peace? I knew I needed to do more than read the Bible and pray. As I reflected on my life in this quest for peace, I realized my greatest joys had always come from helping others. I also knew that giving to others was wonderful in God's eyes.

Whether coaching or just talking with a disabled child, I had found that volunteering and helping others always gave meaning to my pain and life experiences. Somehow, it made them worth the struggles. Helping others always helped me. Writing my book and seeking out others with AMC, though pursued to help others, had proved to help me even more.

A recent example of this had taken place when my friend Ray called to say he was working on his master's degree, and wanted to interview me about prejudices toward handicapped people and the struggles of living with disabilities.

I started out doing a favor for someone else, but, after two hours of discussion, I realized that being truthful to Ray about the pain of what I live with had been a great release. Some days it helps just to be able to say, "I hurt."

Being aware of how helping others helped me, and feeling a bit selfish, I was still anxious to help others in my daily life in any way possible. So when my cousin Annie asked me to speak at her place of employment, a drug and alcohol rehabilitation center, I quickly accepted.

Annie had become an excellent counselor after overcoming numerous obstacles in her own struggle with drugs and alcohol. I asked Pam and Charlie, "When you think of Annie, what comes to your mind?" They both laughed and immediately said, "Loud and funny." How wonderful is that? If you met Annie, you'd never forget. Anyone can hear her from blocks away, and her laughter and smile are contagious.

The people at her facility have had a tough time, and Annie felt I could be of some help, especially spiritually. Though I haven't had problems with drugs or alcohol, I have had problems, and it's amazing how most all our problems relate.

At the center, I shared my story of struggles and triumphs, and the significance of support from others. Most important, I shared my faith and the growth that came from having had to overcome obstacles and tragedies. I also shared my day-to-day struggles with fatigue and pain.

I've also talked individually with several people at this facility who are handicapped or deal with chronic pain. One—a gentleman in his forties who had been a tough, macho, bodybuilder, until an accident left him weak and unable to do much physically—was struggling with both pain and self-worth.

We spent many hours together sharing each other's coping abilities. I felt fortunate having had my whole lifetime to deal with my problems; his life had changed in a moment. He seemed to be doing very well dealing with his pain and uncertainty, until the afternoon he showed up, crying, at my front door. I invited him in, and he began expressing his sadness and hopelessness. He was depressed, and his pain was excruciating. He felt useless and could not stop talking about his inability to do anything. Having experienced depression, I understood, and could feel his pain, hurt, and frustration.

After listening for several minutes, I asked him a question to which I already knew the answer: "Do you like and respect me?"

Wiping away his tears, he chuckled and said, "Of course. Why do you think I'm here?"

I then asked, "Can you fold clothes or do the dishes?"

"Yes," he said.

"Well, that's *all* I can do, and some days I can't even do that. Yet, in your mind, I am important."

We all struggle with life, and sometimes it becomes overwhelming. We feel so alone. I have learned that talking and sharing are among the greatest medicines. I have been able to spend time with loved ones who empathize with my troubles and difficulties, and this has been a great blessing. Friends, both past and present, are truly gifts from God.

Don Peterson, one of my wonderful present friends and a distant relative (not unusual in a small town), is a recovering alcoholic who has taught me so much about A.A. and the Twelve Steps. I feel everyone should go through this program, as it helps us look deep into our journey back to a power greater than ourselves. Both Don and I have overcome numerous obstacles and, now, shared many stories of faith. Because of our spiritual growth and the comfort and enjoyment we found in talking about God, we decided to start a group for the same purpose, to meet once a week for an hour. Membership in the "God Squad" is open to anyone. We have no agenda other than sharing our faith, talking about God, and helping one another and ourselves. Now, years later, we have about fifteen people show up every week.

An early member, Bruce, shared the following beautiful story before one of our meetings. He had walked into the dry cleaner's shop and noticed a bird inside. The bird flew into the window, banged its head, and fell to the floor. When the bird regained its composure, it flew again into the window, banged its head, fell to the floor. Over and over the bird did this, until it had no longer had any energy to move.

Bruce then calmly walked over, gently picked up the bird, took it outside, and set it on the ground. The bird slowly began to move, and then flew away.

When the bird had been in the shop, it couldn't see the window, but only beyond the window. It tried again and again to fly—to take care of itself—only to fail. When the bird finally surrendered, he got help and flew again.

A recovering alcoholic is a great example of hitting rock bottom, failing, then, with help from a higher power or God, succeeding and flying again.

This story relates to each of us sometime in our lives. We look so hard right *through* the window that we don't see what is right in front of us. That's where God is. We all need help, and God is always around, ready to listen. We choose when that will be, whether when we are young or old, healthy or dying.

I believe all we need is to surrender. But actually surrendering to God, always, fully trusting in Him, is a different story.

Living in Norton, in the midst of farmland, helped me begin to understand that my life could be compared to a struggling crop. When plants struggle through their growth, they become stronger and produce a better yield. Mighty winds, lack of moisture, and other stresses helped me develop a larger root system, a root system that began with the love, compassion, and empathy of family and friends.

I was now seeing in a new way how my struggles had been an advantage rather than a disadvantage . . . how my greatest education had come from my experiences . . . how the pains, the sadness, and frustrations of life were leading me right where I wanted to go—to more of God's love and peace.

THE CALL TO HOSPICE

Surrendering to and totally trusting in God were easier said than done. So, during prayer one day, I began asking for more faith, even as I realized my journey for peace was already leading me closer to God.

For example, I had found myself understanding the Bible better than ever. Certain verses had begun jumping out at me and making sense, verses like Philippians 4:13: "I can do all things through Christ Who strengthens me." I had practically lived that verse throughout my life, without even knowing it.

One day, while talking to my sister-in-law Carrie on the phone, she asked me to pray for her.

"I will," I said, "and I will pray for God's will."

Carrie said, "No thanks. I want you to pray for Carrie's will." I laughed. Then I prayed for her acceptance of God's will.

Our conversation reminded me that the Lord's Prayer says, "Thy will be done," meaning God's will, not mine. Hearing and understanding His will are much simpler when it also happens to be what I want. But when it's not, following God's will is hard. Pride and ego seem to get in the way.

Later the evening of my conversation with Carrie, I went to the hospital to visit a friend. When I reached the side entrance, I found the door locked. Frustrated, I thought, "Oh God, why is this door locked? Now I have to walk all the way around to the front." I knew there must be a reason, but I was tired and didn't feel like walking any farther. But I did, and when I entered through the front doors and turned the corner, directly in front of me was my friend Jeannie, coming out of a hospital room.

"Well, what are you doing here?" I asked.

Jeannie said, "My mom has been admitted. She had a stroke."

Her mother was a dear friend of my mother, and my mother happened to be out-of-town. With all the new hospital rules, I might never have learned this woman had had a stroke.

Now I knew why the door was locked.

I would visit this lovely lady many times during the next several weeks before she passed away after suffering another stroke. I wasn't there for anything spectacular; I simply offered a smiling face and a little conversation. But none of that would likely have happened if the side door had not been locked.

Because of my conversation with Carrie earlier that day, I was paying more attention to God's will. Now this incident helped me recognize that I still needed a lot of work to trust and listen to His guidance, if my sense of peace and my faith were to be further strengthened.

Not long after, during a trip to the local drugstore, I started to share the story about the lady in white with an employee and friend, Patty. When I saw a gentleman I did not know, sitting nearby and looking at me rather strangely, I felt uncomfortable and stopped telling Patty the story.

A few minutes later, however, I felt strongly that God wanted me to continue. I was hearing and feeling God deep in my soul, in a way impossible to describe. I simply knew He wanted me to continue, and so I did, trusting in God, and with His guidance.

Patty told me she had enjoyed my sharing this wonderful story with her, but I still wasn't sure why I was supposed to tell it at that time. Nevertheless, I felt I had done the right thing.

I walked outside to get into my car, but was stopped by a man's voice: "Excuse me. That story of the angel, was it true?"

"Yes," I told the unknown man I'd seen listening to me.

He then said, "I have never told anyone this story because I thought people would think I was nuts, but I saw an angel when I was almost killed in my car wreck."

I chuckled and said, "Many times I feel like people think I am nuts." I added, "In fact, I think part of the reason spiritual things happen to me is because God knows I have a big mouth and will share these stories with everyone."

He laughed, and we visited for several more minutes. He seemed so relieved finally to be able to share his story with someone. I had never seen this man before and have not seen him since. And that is hard to do in a town of only a few thousand.

This was an incredible experience! I had truly felt God's presence and heard Him in my soul. God had guided me, and even showed me why. He was teaching and I was learning. My faith was strengthening, and I felt the peace developing in myself that I had once seen in Glenn. I now had an even greater desire to hear more from God. Nearly every day, I went into an empty church to speak to and, as important, listen to God.

A CALL

One day, I sat alone in church, reflecting on the three most powerful spiritual experiences in my life—knowing the presence of the lady in white after my car accident, seeing Glenn's peace as he was dying, and feeling my own sense of peace following Richard's death.

These experiences with death, and more, led me to feel I was being called to hospice. So when Amanda, a volunteer coordinator for hospice in northwest Kansas, invited me to a training session, I was eager to get started. Being a hospice volunteer would allow me to help when I felt well enough, and rest when I didn't.

Through hospice training, I got to know some of the nicest people I had ever met, beginning with Amanda, our teacher. Another new recruit, Leslie, and I were excited about our training, but Amanda and two other veteran volunteers, Elaine and Betty, had a peace about them that I do not often see. The love in their hearts is extraordinary; these people truly are a gift from God.

When my training was over and it was time for my first patient, I was excited, nervous, anxious, and emotional as I drove to her house. My goal was to help these dying patients have the most peaceful possible journey to God and the other side, and I knew I needed help, too. I stopped my car for a few minutes, composed my thoughts, and began praying for that help that I might do God's will.

When I arrived at the patient's home, I asked God for a sign, even though I knew God does not have to answer such prayers. "Please," I prayed, "let me know that my doing hospice is your will."

I continued to pray all the way up the front walk. While knocking on the door, I again asked God, "Please, give me a sign."

My hospice patient opened the door, and the first words out of her mouth were, "Oh, God sent me an angel!" I smiled and thanked God, as I knew this was exactly where He wanted me.

This beautiful lady, Dolores, had less than six months to live. She had had a tough life and, long before her cancer, was very bitter and sometimes angry at the world.

However, Dolores was never bitter and angry around me; instead, we always had fun during our many visits. We shared spiritual stories with each other, and lots of laughter, and she always wanted to help me with things in my daily life.

As time went on, I began realizing how easy this hospice stuff was. Listening and sharing and just loving someone was all I had to do.

Dolores loved her cigarettes, and there was no reason to stop smoking now. I entered her house one day while she was smoking *and* breathing oxygen through her nose. I thought, "Oh my God, I hope she doesn't blow us both up."

I kept my distance without letting her know how scared I was. She probably did wonder why I sat across the room from her. When she put the cigarette out, I moved closer and continued my visit. When she decided to light up again, still with the oxygen attached, I decided that day's visit would be a short one.

With help from her doctor, a hospice social worker, a hospice nurse, and numerous friends, Dolores was beginning to accept her life and her approaching death.

One afternoon, as I was getting up to leave, Dolores unexpectedly said, "Ward, I am so thankful to God; I am the happiest I've been in a long time."

God's grace and peace, I thought—how wonderful. As I looked at this beautiful woman in her late sixties, I could see how awesome God is. She enjoyed that same peace I had seen in Glenn. She was now content and ready to move on.

Several years earlier, while I had been lying in bed late one night, I had noticed a light, or flash, streak across my ceiling. I had never seen anything like it, and wondered what it could be.

The next day I learned one of my friends had died in a car accident at the same time I had seen that flash.

I had not forgotten that experience, but also hadn't thought much about it, until now, when I was driving to Charlie's track meet one afternoon, and that same type of light shot across the sky in broad daylight. I immediately remembered the previous incident and hoped no one I knew had just died.

During the track meet, I received a call from Leslie, dear friend and fellow hospice volunteer, informing me that Dolores had passed away. She had died around the same time I had seen that flash across the sky. Was this light a gift from God to help prepare me for her death? I wasn't sure, but it did bring comfort and a sense of peace.

While driving home from the meet, I began reflecting on my relationship with Dolores. I cried tears of sorrow because I would miss her, and tears of thankfulness, for her pain was over. Both sad and happy, I knew God was with me, and my heart warmed as I realized I had done my best to help her through the dying process.

Dolores had wanted to die while still at home, and she had not wanted to greatly inconvenience her children. She accomplished both, and died quite peacefully. I was so honored to be asked by her children to speak at her funeral.

LESSONS ABOUT DEATH

My next hospice patient, in a nearby town, was also dying of cancer. On this case, I would be working with Elaine, one of the veteran volunteers

I had met during training. She was always full of wonderful advice and had helped me a great deal during the learning process.

As we were driving to the patient's house, Elaine said, "Ward, if someone asked you when your mother was pregnant with you, if you were ready for the big world, you'd probably have said no." She continued, "That is kind of what it's like when someone dies, except you're going to a much better place."

When we arrived at the patient's house, I was shocked at the living conditions we found there. I couldn't imagine living this way, let alone dying in these circumstances. However, judging was not why I was there and not why I am telling this story. I was so thankful to God for all I had, and prayed for those who had much less. This family was doing their best with what they had.

Elaine introduced us and began sharing what we, as hospice volunteers, could do for the patient and family. While she got to work helping with dishes and cleaning up around the house, I sat with the patient, who was fairly comfortable, lying in bed in a vegetative state, in a corner of the living room near a big window.

I said a few prayers quietly, and hoped the patient didn't have to suffer much. I felt somewhat helpless but was also learning more about God's love. His will for me was to focus on what I *could* do. I could sit with the patient, talk to her, and pray for her and her loved ones. I could only do a little, but I could "be there" with love, and what is more important than that?

Shortly thereafter, during a meeting of hospice workers, Amanda began our session by asking each of us volunteers to imagine being told we had less than six months to live. Imagine if we were the patients, the ones we went to see. What would we do, and how many things would change? Would recent arguments with family and friends be that important? Would we call our church? What would we need to get done? A couple of my own questions passed through my mind: Am I right with God? Am I truly at peace?

Imagining our own imminent deaths was a great topic, for us volunteers and for each and every one of us. Suddenly, things we think are important are trivial, and the simplest things in life become treasured.

Family and friends are gifts, and we recognize in a new way how important our loved ones are. I have yet to meet a hospice patient who asked me to get all her money from the bank or gather all the awards he had won. They have asked for family, friends, and loved ones.

After doing this exercise for more than an hour, we had a much greater understanding of what it means to live until we die. Facing death enables us to live to the full, appreciating God's gifts and being thankful for what we have.

Another lesson learned was how important it is to accept everyone where they are spiritually. The religious denomination of a patient—Catholic, Lutheran, Mormon, or any other—is not for me to change. I can share my story and my faith if asked. Otherwise, I am to accept and help the patient anyway they would like.

If I were dying, how much spiritual help would someone from another religion bring to me? Probably not much, and I would certainly not convert. Yet, they could still bring love. They could say prayers that were important to me. Likewise, if I am someone's hospice volunteer, I am not there to judge them. I am there for them—not for me. I am to accept them for who they are, and in no way promote a personal agenda. I am not to be self-righteous and closed-minded. I am with them to show love and to make their dying process as easy and comfortable as possible. We are all God's children.

Leslie, not a Catholic, had a devout Catholic patient dying in the hospital. Remembering this woman loved her rosary, Leslie ran to the car and retrieved the rosary, placing it in the hand of her patient as she passed away. What a beautiful gesture on Leslie's part and an example of what hospice is all about. She did everything she could to help her patient die peacefully. This was not about Leslie and her beliefs, but about her love for God and for her patient.

Through volunteering for hospice I was, again, learning and receiving far more than I could ever give, and God was now revealing to me the importance of love. I was seeing and feeling, as well as figuring out, the importance of unconditional love. I now understood that this kind of love was a big reason I had felt such peace after Richard's death.

SEEING FACES

One afternoon, I was again alone in church, praying. Suddenly I noticed the face on the statue of Jesus above the altar. It was beginning to change.

The face kept becoming different faces, none of which I recognized. When I looked away and then back again, the faces were still changing, each one different. I rubbed my eyes, and then checked to see if the other statues throughout the church were also changing. None were.

For more than twenty minutes, I viewed what looked like a movie of different faces. I wasn't scared. In fact, the whole experience was relaxing, calm, peaceful. Finally I asked God, "What am I suppose to understand from these faces?" Within seconds, I felt I was told to look in everyone, with love, for Jesus.

This was so beautiful, so simple, and yet so powerful. And, soon, I truly understood why this had happened.

A friend called me to his house to help an acquaintance with a dying loved one. When I met the acquaintance, I was stunned by her appearance. Run-down and totally distraught, she looked as if life had not been kind. When I shook her hand, the statue of Jesus with the changing faces flashed through my mind, as if God were telling me that *every* person is His child. I was to love this person as much as and, at this moment, more than anyone in my life. I was also reminded God was with me, as I felt my capacity for compassion, empathy, and love magnified.

I immediately tried to console her and listen intently to her problems and concerns. Not only was she losing a very special person in her life, but she was worried about the dying process and the pain of death. Hospice had already been called in, and I assured her they would do a great job managing the pain and would help the family as well as the patient.

For several minutes, I mostly just listened. Then I began sharing some things that might take place during the dying process. "Your dying relative might use a metaphor for traveling, such as 'the boat is here.' This will let you know death is getting close," I said.

The woman immediately started crying uncontrollably. "Oh no, what did I say?" I thought, and then I asked, "What's wrong?"

Wiping away her tears, she said, "Last night my relative said the boat was here."

I could have chosen any metaphor for traveling, but for some reason, I said "boat." At first, she was shocked and overwhelmed, feeling as if God Himself were helping her. And He was. The peace that grew in her throughout the evening was incredible. I was amazed, as all I did was show unconditional love; God clearly did the rest. Her relative went on to die soon after our visit.

Within a week I went to see a hospice patient who had been pretty angry all his life, and even more so since finding out he was dying. I sat down next to the man's bed and he immediately began telling me how alone he felt and how angry he was at God. He was extremely upset.

When I told him that God understood his anger, he became teary-eyed and then began to cry. We spent the next minutes talking about his struggles through life and about his faith. Again, I mostly just listened.

Later during the visit, he began struggling with guilt and was very shaken. Crying and shaking his head, the patient said, "I have done some pretty bad things in my life."

After several seconds of silence, I took his hand and calmly and peacefully told him, "I am not here to judge you. No matter what you've done in your life, I would still be here, and Jesus is a whole lot more loving and caring than I am."

Sometimes we never know what we are to others, but, with love, we can at least be a friend. I truly did not care what this man might have done, even if he were the worst person ever to have lived. He could have done the most horrible things, and I was not going to judge him. Each and every one of us has good inside, and God's love is what I was trying to see in him, and in all people. Here he was—dying, so alone, afraid— and I was not going to abandon him.

Driving home from that visit, an overwhelming sense of love filled my soul as I realized that we have no concept of how powerful God's love is. We can imagine, but His love is inconceivable. Examples of this love were appearing everywhere in my life. Now I wasn't only trying, but felt I was truly beginning to understand His will. I knew that in my search for peace, and in trying to do my best for others and for God, I had discovered the importance of unconditional love.

STORIES OF LIFE & DEATH

My hospice work has brought me closer to God than ever. Many spiritual experiences both guided me and became common occurrences as I tried to live a faith-filled life. Some of those experiences are described in these beautiful stories of patients who touched and helped change my life forever.

PRAYERS AND LAUGHTER

An elderly gentleman in a nursing home, dying of cancer, seemed to be very agitated. He was having trouble relaxing and could not get comfortable, even for a few minutes.

When I first introduced myself, I asked if he would like me to pray the Lord's Prayer with him. He nodded yes. Halfway through the prayer, he fell asleep. From then on, day after day, every time I went to visit, I would pray and he would fall asleep.

He was a little gruff and grouchy, and could be rather ornery at times. However, we connected instantly through his wonderful, dry sense of humor. He always said he didn't remember me or know who I was. One day, when I was talking to a nurse, he yelled, "Hey Ward, who is that lady?" I turned, laughing, and said, "I knew you knew my name." He smiled.

A few weeks later, during the Lord's Prayer, instead of falling asleep, he became agitated and interrupted me. I could not understand what he was saying, so I continued to pray. He looked uncomfortable and again stopped me. He had never done this before, and I wondered what was important enough to persuade him to interrupt something so special to him. Finally, after several tries, I understood. He was saying, "I gotta pee."

I laughed, and went to get the nurse.

While waiting outside this man's room, I noticed another gentleman about thirty feet down the hall. He was sitting in a wheelchair, hunched over, his head tilted to the side, staring into space. I had seen him many times before, as he was my patient's roommate, but had never known if he could talk or understand anything.

As I looked at him, I saw his lips move and, a few seconds later, heard the words, "Come and talk to me." His lips had moved but the voice had come from somewhere else. I immediately walked to him, all the time wondering what had been the source of the words I'd clearly heard. A calm and peaceful presence filled my soul.

He talked very quietly and, at first, was hard to understand. We visited for several minutes, enjoying each other's company. No great revelation was unveiled. This man didn't tell me anything fascinating, give me a cure for a disease, or part the Red Sea. It was just a simple conversation, two people sharing stories at a time their paths happened to cross (with a little help from God). I was again reminded, however, that God is everywhere and in everyone.

When I reentered my patient's room, he asked if I would finish praying with him, and, before I was done with the Lord's Prayer, he was fast asleep. At that point, two nurses walked in to say a resident across the hall would like to see me.

I walked into her room. There lay a beautiful eighty-five-year-old woman, all tucked in bed, wearing a pink nightcap to keep her head warm. I introduced myself and she thanked me for coming over. Then she said, "I have heard you pray with that man across the hall many times. The Lord's Prayer is my favorite, and I love your voice. Would you pray with me, too?" I almost cried as we began, "Our Father, who art in heaven . . . ." She was so happy that we prayed it again, and I told her I would come back.

This was the simplest thing I had ever done, and yet I felt as if I had done one of the most important things ever. Every evening from then on, while I visited my hospice patient, this lady would sit in her wheelchair outside the door, and let me know when she was going to bed, so I could pray with her.

By the way, my ornery hospice patient, whom I dearly loved, got the last laugh. He died on National Grouch Day.

I continue to visit and pray with this eighty-five-year-old lady a few times each week. Most of the time she doesn't even remember my name, but she always knows we pray together. Every time I leave, before I am five steps from her room, I hear her tell her roommate, "I just love that young man." Not much can make me feel better.

THE RIGHT PLACE AT THE RIGHT TIME

My dad had asked me to visit a friend of his in the hospital, an elderly woman who hadn't been feeling well. There was no hurry, and he just wanted me stop by the next time I was in the area.

About to leave the hospital one morning, I remembered my dad's request. So I went back down the hall and into his friend's room, said hello, and introduced myself. She was happy to meet me and said, "What perfect timing. My doctor just left the room after telling me I have cancer. I am going to die."

I said, "Oh, I am so sorry."

I was again amazed. God had put me in her room at that exact moment. With my hospice training and experience, I didn't have all the answers, but I knew I could sit, visit, hold her hand, and just listen.

Audrey, a beautiful eighty-four-year-old woman originally from Arkansas, smiled and said, "I have had a great life, and I'll be fine."

I was impressed with the peace she had, and I told her I would be back to visit. "Please call me anytime for anything," I said. We were friends instantly.

The following evening, Audrey's daughter Diana called to thank me for visiting her mom. Diana said, "She told me about a visit from a nice young man named Ward, and she was in love." (I use that line often when I do speeches, especially when my wife is in the audience.)

Audrey went home to stay with her daughter for several weeks. One beautiful afternoon I sat in the back bedroom with her, talking about our faith and sharing spiritual stories. The room suddenly became very still, and we could feel a calm and peaceful presence, a presence of comfort, reminding me of the feeling I had had with the lady in white, and the calm feeling I'd experienced sitting alone in church watching Jesus's face changing. It was beautiful and pure. I can't even begin to describe the feeling, except to say that it was total love.

Audrey was now much weaker than when we had met. Our conversation was serious and very emotional. I listened intently as she said, "When I die, I sure hope I go to the right place."

"Oh, I am sure you will."

In her Arkansas accent she answered, with a serious voice, "No, you don't understand. I don't do well in heat."

I burst out laughing and was again impressed with this remarkable woman. Here I was trying to help her, and she—dying—was teaching and comforting me with her wonderful sense of humor.

Our friendship grew, and we could talk about anything. On another occasion I said, "Audrey, when you die, put a good word in for me."

Without hesitating she said, "You want me to lie to God?"

A few weeks later, Audrey, still weaker, asked to go back to the hospital. She was ready and did not want to die at home.

The following day, I visited her there, where she was resting comfortably.

"How are you doing?" I asked.

Audrey was excitedly waiting to graduate from this world, so said, "Well, I am still here. Why haven't I gone yet?"

I chuckled and said, "I'm not sure, Audrey. Maybe because it's Valentines Day?"

"Oh, okay," she calmly answered. In the early morning hours of February 15, this wonderful lady went home to be with God. She had died how she lived, very peacefully.

COUNTING THE ANGELS

Late one evening, I headed to the nursing home, where another hospice patient was close to death. I sat quietly with him, praying, and felt sure he was going to pass away soon.

The patient, in fact, had been ready to die for weeks and couldn't understand why he hadn't. "God's time, not ours," I would tell him.

He looked peaceful and comfortable and all signs pointed to him leaving us during the night. Things quickly changed as the patient began looking irritated. He was staring at something the nurse and I couldn't see. Suddenly he looked sad and a few tears began to roll down his cheeks.

"What's wrong?" I asked.

He wouldn't answer and kept looking elsewhere as tears continued down his face.

I again asked, "What's wrong?"

He then, very sadly, said, "I can't go yet. It's not my time."

Even though many of us had thought he would pass on that night, he was right. For some reason, it wasn't his time and he knew it.

For the next few days, it seemed this patient was working things out by talking to people who weren't visible. A few times he got angry; once he even yelled, "Go to hell." I hoped he wasn't talking to me. I guess not, as a couple of minutes later, he calmly said, "Let's pray."

A week after the night we thought he would die, I again sat quietly next to his bed, listening to music. I heard him try to say something, but didn't understand.

"I'm right here. What do you need?"

A nurse walked into the room as he said, "I am not talking to you. I am talking to the angels."

The nurse asked him, "How many angels do you see?"

"There are too many to count. They are everywhere."

"Wow," I thought. "How beautiful."

A peaceful and calm presence filled the room, wonderful and, again, indescribable. The patient died peacefully, soon after this experience.

THE LOOK OF LOVE

I was at the nursing home when an aide told me a resident would like a visitor. The aide asked me to see, and maybe even pray with, Sandy, a woman dying of cancer. Sandy and I did pray together several times, but most of my visits were short. Often I would just pray quietly while she slept.

A few weeks later, while I was at the home visiting another patient, a nurse told me Sandy was "out of it" and nearing death, and asked if I would please make sure to see her before I left.

Sandy looked weak and almost comatose as I sat down next to her bed and began praying silently for her. I also asked God if I had done well. I hoped I had helped Sandy in a small way.

After several minutes of prayer, I whispered her name and said I was leaving. That familiar calm and loving presence filled the room as Sandy opened her eyes, and smiled as beautiful a smile as I had ever seen. She grabbed my hand and looked at me like no one had ever looked at me before. She seemed to see right through me, finding only whatever was good.

I told her I would pray for her. She smiled even bigger, and with a heart so warm. She tried to talk, but not much came out. I asked if she'd like me to pray for her now, and she smiled again, with a little nod. While holding her hands, I began praying the Lord's Prayer as she continued to look at me with love.

When I got up to leave, Sandy took both of my hands, squeezing as tightly as she could. With all her strength, she pulled me closer until my face was only inches from hers. I thought she was going to speak, and she tried, but couldn't. So with her beautiful smile and her eyes wide, she took her right hand and, ever so gently, patted my left cheek three times.

Everything she wanted to say, I heard through her love and those three little pats.

"God bless you, and I will continue to pray for you," I said. "God bless you." I started to say, "I will see you soon," but stopped because I knew this was all for her. Sandy died, very peacefully, with her family present, two days later.

A TOUCH OF HOME

I had grown so much since I had seen in Glenn the peace that I searched and longed for. Through praying and reading the Bible, surrendering to and trusting in God, listening and following His will, I was now living with that peace more than ever.

Amanda called and asked if I would see a new hospice patient at the hospital. This woman was having a tough time with dying and leaving her grandchildren, and she was also not talking much. She was very depressed, a condition I used to think would be common for those dying, but had learned was not always the case.

I was told she would not talk to anyone and was giving the nurses a hard time. She seemed to be angry at nearly everybody, and was obviously frustrated with many issues, issues I hoped could be worked out before she died.

I walked into her room and introduced myself. She was shy, and turned away, not wanting to talk. So I began telling her some stories of my life and faith. She acted as if she didn't care, ignoring me, doing a crossword puzzle. Many times she would answer my questions with only a single word; sometimes she would not answer at all. But I felt I was where God wanted me to be, so I basically began doing a speech. I've never had a problem talking, and this was no exception.

Normally, I would have left, as it seemed clear she didn't want me around, but I felt strongly I should keep talking. So I did. Trusting God's guidance, I continued for nearly thirty minutes. I prayed silently between stories.

All of a sudden, she spoke. "Sacramento is where you're from?"

"Yes, I grew up and had most of my surgeries done in Sacramento," I said. God had connected us through the place I was born and raised. She had lived in Sacramento for awhile. Suddenly I was all right in her eyes, and she began talking and sharing.

We then visited on numerous occasions. I often felt she even looked forward to my visits. She did seem to find that peace we all search for, and I felt honored when she passed away on my birthday.

PERFECT TIMING

On another occasion, Amanda called and said we had a new patient, an older gentleman with cancer. He was in the hospital and needed someone to sit with him. Amanda said he was getting close to death, that he was all alone, and didn't have any family.

I immediately drove to the hospital, entered the room, and introduced myself. He couldn't talk, but I felt he understood who I was. I visited with him several times a day, even if it was only for a little while. I just sat quietly, sometimes talking to him and sometimes praying.

I remember asking God one day, why I was with this patient. I knew I might never know, and I was content simply sitting with this man so he wasn't alone. But I am never afraid to ask God anything. I may not get answers, but I can ask.

The next day, during another visit with the same man, I again asked God what I was to do and why I was there. Within minutes, in walked three adults.

I said hello, and introduced myself. They did the same, and then one said, "We have just driven more than six hours to be with our father."

I thought, "Your father? I didn't think he had any family."

This was incredible. We talked for a few minutes and then I left, to give them time alone. However, first I offered them my telephone number. The patient was too weak to hold the phone or even talk, so I told them to feel free to call me anytime, and I would come to the hospital to hold the phone to their father's ear whenever they wished to speak to him.

God, again, had answered my questions. These children had thought their father was dying alone, and they were so thankful someone was sitting with him. Such gratitude for such an easy thing for me to do! For me to be with their father when they walked through the hospital door, was beautiful and perfect timing. I thanked God for answering another of my questions with an explanation, but knew this wouldn't always happen. I needed to remember to trust in Him whether I knew why or not.

MORE GIFTS

A few days later, my phone rang at 4:00 A.M. When I answered, Amanda said, "I'm sorry for calling at this hour, but can you go to the hospital? We have a patient dying, and it looks like she might pass away soon."

I immediately drove to the hospital. The patient, in her sixties, was in a comatose state and looked comfortable. Her husband was sitting at her bedside when I arrived.

I introduced myself and sat in a chair on the other side of the bed. I didn't do much except listen and be present. As I had already learned, sometimes the most important thing to do is nothing, just "be there." This was one of those occasions.

Mid-morning, the patient died. I could see in her husband's eyes the love they had had for one another, and his terrible feeling of loss. His best friend had died, and he was alone, as their children lived in other parts of the country. I was happy I was able to be with him.

Although he continued to be upset, I felt he had calmed down enough that he would be all right while I went home to get some rest.

A few hours later, I went out again, to run errands. As I did, three different people came up and thanked me for helping this gentleman in his time of great loss.

Confidentiality is very important in hospice work, especially in a small town, so I wondered how these people even knew I had been with him. Then I learned this gentleman was so grateful for my "being there," he was apparently telling everyone in town.

Though I do hospice because of my faith in God and the belief I am doing His will, it was still nice to hear other people being thankful and appreciative. This is not something to which hospice volunteers are accustomed.

The next week, I attended the woman's funeral in a church I had attended only once before. I found a seat in a middle pew, and was daydreaming a bit while the minister spoke. I perked up, however, when I heard my name mentioned. The minister pointed to me and said, "That is exactly where the patient sat every Sunday for church."

I was sitting in her usual seat. "Wow," I thought. With all the places there were to sit, I chose the spot in which she had sat for years. Incredible and amazing! Was this a sign? Was God speaking to me again? Maybe, maybe not. But it did get me to pay more attention to the service!

Now I realized, in a new way, that each step I took toward God seemed to result in His showering me with gifts—of growth, understanding, acceptance, and most important, love. So much love. And, as always, though I was giving, God was blessing me far more.

Just simple prayers with others had brought me great joy. When a man needed a visitor and couldn't speak loud enough to ask, God spoke, sending me his way. While sitting in a room with Audrey and while hearing a man talk of angels, I felt the peaceful presence of God, that presence of total love, the same gift I had felt through three little pats on my cheek. God had connected me to someone through the town in which we had both lived. God had answered my questions when I was unsure.

I had prayed for my faith to be strengthened, and it has been. It's a gift I now unwrap and cherish daily.

SIGNS

Twenty years after my cousin Annie lost her father to cancer on Christ-mas Eve, she and her sixteen-year-old son were decorating the front door of their modest apartment. As they worked, she shared memories of her father with Christopher, who had never met his grandfather. She also talked about her drug and alcohol abuse, about how horrible she felt about things she had put him through, and how proud she was of him and his efforts in life.

This was the most intense, spiritual, and beautiful evening she and her son had ever spent together. Tears of forgiveness and love flowed throughout the evening.

When they were done, the front door had been decorated with Christ-mas lights her father had used. Both of them were proud of their work, and especially of the love they had been able to show one another. And Annie was so thankful to God for taking care of her children and keep-ing her alive through the most horrible of experiences.

Christopher went into the house, grabbed the camera, and brought it out to his mom, saying, "Let's take a picture of the Christmas lights on the front door." He did not ever want to forget this evening.

A few days later, Annie picked up the film on her way home, then began glancing through the pictures as she sat at the kitchen table. When she saw the one of the front door, she yelled, "Christopher, come here! You won't believe this."

On the picture of the front door could be seen a translucent angel blowing a trumpet. Both clearly saw this beautiful miracle, and had no need for explanations and proof. They were both thankful to God.

Many were astounded and amazed by this picture, and, if I hadn't seen it with my own eyes, I wouldn't have believed it existed. Annie would not sell the picture, but she did make copies for many of her friends, and for me, and told its story only to those she felt God wanted to know.

Several years later, Annie was now also living in Norton. My phone rang at 12:30 A.M. and, half asleep, I answered. An anxious and excited Annie began yelling, "Wardie, Wardie, my angel is on the wall!"

"What?" I said. "What are you talking about?"

"The angel from my picture . . . it is on the wall right here in my bedroom!"

Wondering if Annie was again on drugs or losing her mind, I told her to get her seventeen-year-old daughter Julia to come into her room, to find out if she could see the angel.

I stayed on the phone with her. Then I heard Julia say, "Mom, it's your angel!"

Annie described the angel as about three feet by three feet (the size of a poster), a beautiful sky blue, and blowing a trumpet. The image and shape were the exact form of the angel on the Christmas picture from years earlier. I told Annie I would be over in the morning.

I woke up early, and immediately headed to Annie's house. When I entered her room, I was stunned by what I saw. The angel on the wall was exactly the same as the angel in the picture, except that the picture's angel had been clear or white. Now, on the wall, the angel was sky blue and, of course, bigger.

I told a hospice patient about the angel, and she asked me to take her to see Annie's wall. Also wanting to see the angel were my cousins Dave and Donna, parents of my namesake Matt, whom they had lost at age twelve. They had recently adopted six-year-old Jaclynn, a distant relative who had lost her mother a few months earlier in a car accident. So we arranged a time for all of us to meet at Annie's.

That evening, my hospice patient, her forty-five-year-old son, my cousins, their new little girl, and I gathered in Annie's back bedroom and stared in awe at what we were seeing.

Suddenly, Jaclynn said to my hospice patient, "Hey, this angel has come to get you."

Completely shocked, I wanted to tell her to be quiet. But I kept my mouth shut.

Jaclynn then said, "My mom died, and I know this angel is here to get you."

I could not believe what I was hearing. This little girl was so matter-of-fact, acting as if she knew what was going on.

A few moments later, Jaclynn put her hand on the angel on the wall, and said, "Look, my hand is glowing."

Her hand, pressed against the wall, was illuminated all around her fingers. When she moved it slowly across the wall, a trail of her fingers remained visible for a few seconds, and then the original appearance of the angel returned.

She was so young, and yet so old and wise. I could not believe what I was seeing. Jaclynn and my hospice patient had connected so strongly; the peace in their eyes was beautiful.

The angel remained on the wall for more than three months, and more than one hundred people saw this gift. Then came the day when my hospice patient died very peacefully. Within a few hours of her death, the angel on the wall disappeared.

Jaclynn had been right, and smarter than all the rest of us. I have noticed that the innocence of children and their acceptance of God does sometimes allow them to see and understand much more than adults do.

Who was the angel for? Clearly, it was for my hospice patient, but also for Jaclynn, Annie, Dave, Donna, and all who experienced this gift of love.

Why did the angel appear on the wall? It truly does not matter to me, and explaining the incident, trying to figure it out, or proving it happened, are not important either.

"How do you know it's of God?" someone asked. I just know. That's not an answer most people would or should use to persuade someone to accept something. But, trying to convince someone of the truth of this experience is not important to me either. Some of my most powerful spiritual experiences—the lady in white, the flash across the sky, Jesus's face changing in church, and this angel on the wall—had many things in common. Besides being absolutely amazing, they brought a comfort, peace, and, most important, love. These experiences strengthened my faith and continue to lead me to want even more of God in my life.

I heard a priest once say that part of judging if a miracle took place is how it changed the person involved. How could anything that makes us thankful, and brings us to God and everlasting peace, ever be wrong?

SICKNESS AND HEALTH

Meanwhile, Dad and Mom had been spending a lot of time in Denver seeing doctors. Dad had been sick; now they discovered he had a form of lung cancer. We were all worried as doctors operated right away, removing half of Dad's lung.

He came through the surgery fine, and we were so relieved. Soon, he was back having coffee with his buddies, and, other than occasionally using an oxygen machine, he seemed as normal as ever.

However, Dad recovered just in time for Mom to be diagnosed with a cancer of her own, Non-Hodgkin's lymphoma. Mom and Dad were back in Denver.

Her treatment began with a nine-hour back fusion surgery. Then came chemotherapy. Mom suffered a great deal during the next weeks and months. Losing weight and all her hair were nothing compared to the pain she endured throughout her treatment.

Seeing my mother go through all this was very difficult. After all, she wasn't supposed to be sick. She was the one in charge of everything, the one who made my tough times easier to handle. Mom took care of me, and always made everything all right.

Finally, Mom made it through her last chemo treatment. She was so excited at beating the odds and surviving cancer, and couldn't wait to finally get home. She was going to be able to attend her first grandchild's wedding. Kirk's daughter Megan was getting married, and Mom was so excited. She would have liked to cater the whole affair, but, at this point, the thought of just being there was wonderful.

Very early one morning, Craig and I began our drive to Denver to help mom and dad get home. We missed a turn six miles out-of-town that set us back about ten minutes. An hour later, a huge white bird flew into my windshield, slowing us down again. "Do you think God is trying to tell us something?" I asked.

Another hour passed, and the weather changed drastically. In fact, though it was May, it had started snowing. Once again we had to slow down. Craig and I just took these as signs to enjoy the drive, take our time, and be safe.

We eventually made it to my Aunt Patsy's house. She and Aunt Dorothy had helped Mom immensely through the hard year. They had been nurses, counselors, friends, and wonderful sisters. Mom had a hard time saying goodbye to them, but she also couldn't wait to get home. Craig drove Mom and Dad in their car; I followed in mine.

Mom was still very weak, and I prayed the whole way home that this five-hour trip would go well, and that she would be comfortable. Two hours into the trip, my cell phone rang. It was Dad in the car ahead, saying we needed to take the next exit so Mom could use the restroom.

Everything went well, to my relief. Craig and Dad pushed Mom in the wheelchair into the handicapped accessible bathroom. I got a soda and candy, and visited with everyone while I waited.

When Mom came out, she was her old self, trying to buy us hot dogs, chips, and various other treats for the rest of the journey home. (Of course, I grabbed some more snacks, just to make Mom feel better.)

We made it home safely a few hours later. As we pulled into the driveway, we immediately noticed the grandkids' "Welcome Home" signs on the house. Mom could not have been happier to be home after her hard-fought battle against cancer.

A few days later, some of Mom's good friends from California showed up in Norton. Virginia, Anna Beth, Pat, and Jeanette drove halfway across the country to spend time with her. We all laughed and shared wonderful memories. Despite her continuing weakness and having to spend most of her time in bed, Mom still tried to entertain her friends by having meals brought in. No matter how tired Mom became, she never wanted anyone to leave or the fun to end.

Then Megan and Robbie's wedding arrived, and Mom's daughters-in-law helped her get dressed. She looked so beautiful, and she had accomplished her goal. She was able to attend Megan's wedding.

VACATION

About that same time, Donna and the kids and I headed to California for vacation, to visit Donna's mother and Chris's family, and so Charlie could attend a kicking camp.

Back when Charlie was in fourth grade, he started wanting to play football, and Donna, afraid he would get hurt, told him no. That very evening, I took him out in the backyard and began teaching him how to kick.

I remember telling him that 90 percent of kicking is in the mind. I didn't really know much about kicking, but thought he could learn the best way by practicing. For several weeks, he couldn't get the ball over our five-foot fence. When he finally managed that, he moved his practice into the street.

Finally, in fifth grade, Charlie kicked the ball over the goal post, scoring a fifteen-yard field goal. We were so excited to see his progress.

Charlie continued to practice, and he was a sophomore in high school when all that hard work and perseverance paid off.

Norton's varsity football team was playing one of its biggest rivals. Down by three points with five seconds left in the game, we'd moved the ball to the fifteen-yard line. Then Coach Graber yelled Charlie's name and sent him in to try for a field goal.

A proud dad, I stood on the sideline with hundreds of other spectators and hoped he would just kick the ball like he had done thousands of times before.

Charlie ran out on the field and set the tee on the twenty-yard line—only five yards from the ball when it should have been seven. I screamed to get his attention, to no avail. "Oh no, his kick is going to be blocked," I thought. I knew how nervous he must be, to make such a mistake.

The center hiked the ball, and the holder caught and set it on the tee perfectly. Charlie took his two steps and kicked from the twenty-yard line. Time ran out, the referee blew his whistle, and then held both arms straight up in the air. The crowd cheered. Charlie had made the field goal and sent the game into overtime! We went on to win by seven points.

Charlie became an all-state kicker because of his many hours of hard work, but the best part of this story is not his kicking success, but the memories made and the bonding between father and son because of the time we had spent together.

Donna's mother, Jean, and Jean's boyfriend, Ray, met us in Tahoe for the two-day kicking camp. We then spent several more days with them in the San Francisco area. I also drove to Sacramento for a day to meet my boyhood friend, Andy, and give a speech at the grade school I had attended more than twenty-five years earlier.

Just as I was about to begin, four of my mom's old friends surprised me by walking into the auditorium. Edie, Anna Beth, Vi, and Pat had watched me grow up, and had given me so much love and support throughout my life. I was so thrilled by this wonderful gesture. And this was to be the last time I saw the wonderful lady we all called Mrs. Edie; she passed away within two months.

But the highlight of my speech came after it was over, when I met a second-grader born with AMC. I couldn't believe another boy with the same rare condition was attending "my" school. We shared many stories that happy day.

Our time in California ended with a few days visiting Chris and his family. Once more, we were taken to nice restaurants and treated like royalty. After a wonderful vacation, we headed home.

There we learned Mom had just been admitted to the Norton County Hospital.

SAYING GOODBYE

Dad and I were sitting on either side of my mother's bed a few days later when her doctor walked into the room to tell us the cancer was back. He said, "I am so sorry, Joan, but there is no more treatment that will help."

It was as if someone had punched me in the gut. Time stopped. My heart began to pound. I wanted to scream. This was my mom! How could it be true?

The doctor again said he was sorry and told us hospice could be called in if we'd like.

We all began trying to comfort each other. We were devastated, and there was nothing I could say. We cried as I held Mom's hand and rubbed her leg. Mom had fought so hard and so long, and now she was going to die.

The greatest person in my life was leaving, and there was nothing I could do. The woman who gave birth to me, who held my hand at every surgery and loved me more than anyone else, was going to die. All the treatment did not work. All her suffering and pain was for naught. The lady who prayed for me, and loved me no matter what I did, was dying. There are not enough ways or words to express the love my mom showed me throughout my life. This was one of the worst days of my life.

Since the day I was born, my mom had taught me about Jesus and faith, and to always try to look for the good in everything. How could I ever see any good in this? Again I was being reminded that, just because I had been through a lot in my life, I wasn't exempt from more bad things happening. And all the physical pain couldn't compare to the loss I was about to experience.

LIFE GOES ON

Amanda called to ask how I was doing. She was not only my hospice supervisor, but a dear friend. We visited about my mother for awhile, and I suggested that Betty and Leslie be her hospice volunteers, though anyone would have been great. I have never met a hospice volunteer I didn't love.

But I knew Leslie and Betty could bring their love and wonderful personalities to my mother. Each would bring their special gifts from God to help my mom through her dying process. I also knew they would share their warmth and love with my family members, as well as being there for me.

During our conversation, Amanda asked if I would mind visiting a hospice patient down the hall from my mom. I often teased Amanda later about having me do hospice work when my mom was dying. But Amanda knew me well, and knew this was what I wanted, and that my faith would carry me through. "Of course I will," I told Amanda.

I didn't know much about this older lady, and that is the way I liked it. I only wanted to know what I had to about each patient. Then I could get to know that person myself, without preconceived ideas, and learn who they were through their own words. The next day, I found her room and introduced myself. She immediately said, "You need to get a haircut."

I laughed because that is what my mom told me every time I saw her. This lady then said, "No, you'd better not, because then I might not recognize you." After a short but lovely visit, I said goodbye and told her I would see her again soon.

The next day I stopped into her room for another visit and found two adults standing and staring at this lovely lady. The patient looked as if she had failed since the day before, and I wondered if she had gone into a comatose state. I introduced myself to the two visitors, who told me they were her children.

The patient heard me talking, opened her eyes, and said, with an upbeat voice, "You're back." She then grabbed my hand, kissed it, and pulled me down toward her, and kissed me on the cheek. I felt wonderful, although a little guilty as well. She wasn't even talking to her own children.

I discovered later, from Amanda, that the patient's children learned from the way I acted toward their mother, and were eventually more able to talk with their mom.

THE FAMILY GATHERS

With the arrival from California of Chris and Carrie and their four children, the Foley family was now all together in Norton. We took turns spending time with Mom, and then everyone would meet in her hospital room for dinner. Dad, the four of us boys, our wives, and all the grandchildren spent every night laughing, reminiscing, and sharing.

And every evening, Mom would take money out of her purse and send the grandchildren on an errand for her—to get ice cream for us all. Even on her deathbed, she continued to make sure everyone was having fun, especially her precious grandchildren.

One evening Mom, still mostly bald from her chemotherapy, looked into a mirror across the room from her bed, and said, "Isn't my hair just beautiful and coming back so nicely?"

I almost burst out laughing, but then realized she wasn't joking. "Yes, Mom, your hair looks nice," I said.

To Mom, her hair was as beautiful as it had been when she was younger, and this is not uncommon with hospice patients. On other occasions, Mom talked to people no one else could see. She would be carrying on a conversation with us, turn her head toward what we thought was nothing, talk a few seconds, and then come right back to our conversation.

More than anything, Mom loved being together with family and friends. Dad very seldom left Mom's bedside. Mom's brother Jack, his wife Esther, and Mom's sister Nadyne were at the hospital nearly every day. So many visitors passed in and out, the Norton Hospital must have thought it was a convenience store.

The whole staff was wonderful and always attentive to our needs. I did wonder once why Gary, Kelli, Jennifer, and the rest of the nurses came to see Mom so often; then I noticed the big bowl of candy Mom had sitting next to her bed. All the nurses were exceptional and very caring, and that made our sorrow easier to deal with.

Mom loved living more than anyone I knew. She hated leaving all of us. But she was now getting ready to move on.

Chris had visited Mom throughout her year in Denver and a number of times in Norton, too. Now he had run out of vacation and had to head back to California, but, before he left, Mom wanted one last meeting with all of her boys.

A few days earlier, a minister friend had told me that seeing 111 or 1111 was a sign that God's angels were present. I laughed when he told me, yet still stashed the thought away in the back of my mind, knowing there was no harm in anything that reminded me of being thankful to God. Since then, I have heard other people say you should make a wish when you see ones, but I still like to think of it as a reminder of God and His angels.

The night before Chris was to leave, we four boys gathered in Mom's room for one last time together. We huddled around her bed, sharing stories and memories. Kirk even said something rather profound, surprising me a great deal. He said, "Mom, when you get to heaven, it might only be a couple of seconds before we are all with you." (Assuming Kirk goes to heaven.) How right he was, as eternity has no time, and, for her, we will all be there in the blink of an eye.

For several hours, we laughed and cried and said goodbye and thanked one another. We shared a beautiful evening together.

When I got home, emotionally spent, I sat on the couch and reflected on the wonderful evening, and I thanked God for giving us this time with our mother.

On my way to bed, I walked into the kitchen to get some water and happened to glance at the VCR. Its clock read 11:11. I thanked God again and slept peacefully through the night.

Chris left for home, but Carrie and the kids stayed in Norton. The older grandkids baby-sat the younger so Carrie could help Mom do things she needed to get done.

For example, though it was only June, Mom wanted all the Christmas presents bought and wrapped. She also wrote letters to all her friends and needed numerous other errands run. Mom was dying the way she had lived her life, thinking of others.

THE ANGEL BALLOON

One Saturday morning I walked into Mom's room for a visit. Unexpectedly upbeat, she said, "Hi, Ward! Look at my angel balloon."

This was an average-sized yellow balloon with a big smiley face on it. A confused look on my face, I glanced at Craig and Anna, who were visiting, and said, "What?"

Mom continued, "When I was eating my breakfast, I thought someone was staring at me from the corner of the room. When I looked up, my balloon headed out of the room and down the hallway. I had to call the nurses to retrieve it."

"This balloon is an angel?"

The balloon then started moving from where Anna was sitting to Mom in bed, then from Mom to Anna, and back again to Mom.

"Wow," I thought. Chuckling, I said, "Craig, if this is an angel balloon, you must feel horrible, because I haven't seen it anywhere near you."

Everyone laughed. The balloon immediately traveled from Mom, over Anna's head, to where Craig was sitting. It stopped three feet from his head, the smiley face staring right at him.

"Whoa," I said, and sat down. As soon as I did, the balloon came over to me and hovered next to my shoulder for several minutes. I said, "This balloon must be happy I am sitting down."

The balloon then moved to Mom's dinner table. There it dropped a couple of feet and planted itself underneath. Within a minute, the nurse brought in Mom's lunch. We all laughed, and spent a fun and peaceful morning talking about spiritual stories.

I went home and called Aunt Mary Kay to tell her about the balloon, then went to Annie's, sharing the story with her, too, while we drove to the hospital. After all, Annie had been the one who had sent the balloon to Mom more than two weeks before.

When Annie and I walked into the hospital room, the balloon immediately traveled across the room, and hovered one foot above Annie's head. Completely amazed, Annie laughed as only Annie can, waking up any patients who might already have settled down for an afternoon nap.

I said, "The angel balloon must be happy I brought you here, Annie."

Suddenly, the balloon traveled to where I was sitting, dropped down more than three feet, and turned so its smiley "mouth" gently touched my cheek as if it were giving me a kiss. Carrie took a picture of the balloon just after it "kissed" me.

Later that day, Mary Kay and Jack and their son Michael came to visit Mom. Mary Kay hadn't told Jack anything about the balloon, wanting to see what would happen and hear his explanation.

Jack, a physicist, and a man with an explanation for everything, noticed the balloon kept flying out of the room. Michael would retrieve it, but the balloon, again and again, flew out of the room. As Michael brought the balloon back for the fourth time, Jack said, "Wow, you sure can tell which way the wind current is moving in this room."

Seconds later, the balloon traveled across the room, dropped a couple of feet, and stopped, the face staring directly at Jack. Less than a foot from his face and several feet off the ground, in midair, the balloon planted itself for more than ten minutes, never taking its "eyes" off Jack.

Jack didn't say a word. Mom and Mary Kay just smiled at each other.

When the time came to leave, Jack said, "Mary Kay, there is something very special about that balloon."

The next day, Leslie came to visit mom. She had heard from me about the balloon and looked for it as she entered the room, but it was nowhere to be seen.

Leslie sat on the bed, prayed, and visited with Mom for about a half-hour. When she got up to leave, the balloon was on the bed right next to them.

Family and friends discussed the unusual behavior of this balloon many times, and the conversation always turned to God and faith. This balloon was certainly remarkable, yet we were unsure why and how it did what it did. These things, however, were not necessarily for us to understand. I knew I needed just to be thankful to God, for that balloon had brought us all closer to Him while strengthening our faith and bringing us comfort.

A LAST GOODBYE

We had a new dog, Ginger, a little more than a year old. She was a lot of work, but training her to sleep in a kennel at night was going well. On July 7, however, I was awakened by the dog at about 5:00 A.M. For the first time ever, I had forgotten to put Ginger in the kennel before going to bed.

Fortunately, nothing in the house had been destroyed. The only harm done was that I was wide-awake and couldn't go back to sleep. So I took a shower, got dressed, and went to the hospital to relieve my dad and allow him some much-needed rest.

For several hours I prayed and talked to Mom, now in a comatose state. She didn't move at all, just lay there, barely breathing.

Once I said, "Mom, try to relax." Then I laughed and said, "I know, that's easy for me to say." Mom groaned, but with a chuckle, and I knew then she could hear me. I'd learned in my hospice training that hearing is often one of the last senses to go.

I continued to pray, sometimes quietly and sometimes aloud. I thanked my mom numerous times for all she had done for me. I reminisced about my childhood and told her how much I would miss her but that I would be okay.

Other than that brief groan, Mom had not responded for several hours. I took her hand and told her how much I loved her. She slowly removed her hand from my grasp, and, instead, dropped it on top of mine, squeezing her fingers. She was holding my hand. I was so moved; tears began to roll down my cheeks.

Still praying, I thought how nice it would be if Leslie were here, too. God answered this prayer, as, soon, Leslie walked through the door. She and I talked for a few minutes, and then we prayed together and with Mom. We had a very peaceful time and, just as our prayers came to an end, Dad returned.

A little while later, around noon, I told Mom once again how much I loved her and then went home, leaving Leslie with my mother and father.

Within an hour, I got the call. Mom had passed away. The woman who had stayed up all night praying for me on the day I was born, and who prayed for me every day since, was now dead. Mom had held my hand throughout my life and even in her death. *Thank you, Lord, for this wonderful Lady.*

COWBELLS & SMILEY FACES

The new priest, Father Vincent, came to help make the necessary arrangements. He asked if any of us would like to speak at the service.

I felt I had to speak at my mother's funeral. All she had done for me . . . I had to. And speaking in public was one of the things in life I was pretty good at. Mom's eulogy, however, would be the hardest speech I ever gave.

On July 11, four days after my mother's death (and one day after Chris's birthday), the time arrived.

I had prayed, and I had practiced my speech every chance I had. I wanted so badly to do the tribute well. I wanted to make it through the whole speech without crying. Not that crying would be so bad, but I was afraid I wouldn't be able to stop once I started. Megan's husband, Robbie, helped ease my mind when he offered to be on standby in case I couldn't finish.

This funeral was as beautiful as it could be. Craig's daughter Erin sang wonderfully, and the high school band teacher, our friend David Will, sang Mom's favorite song, "Ave Maria." Chris did a wonderful job reading from the Bible, except that he omitted two sentences he didn't like.

"It's too negative for Mom's funeral," Chris had said.

"You can't just edit the Bible," I answered.

Chris stuck to his guns: "A reading is already an edited version of the Bible. I am just editing a little more."

I thought, "And I'm the one in bad standing with the church!"

Megan spoke beautiful words with a bit of humor, and then it was my turn. I prayed silently as I approached the lectern.

The church was packed. I glanced at the crowd and saw Donna, my aunts and uncles, nieces and nephews. Many of them smiled, trying to bring comfort, and help me relax. Dad looked tired; Kirk and Craig were bent over, their heads in their hands; Chris nodded, wishing me well.

I began by inviting everyone to dinner following the burial. This helped me relax and focus. I glanced down at my notes and prayed one more prayer: "Here goes, Lord. Please help me."

My mom's key to life was Faith, Family, and Friends.

Mom gave everything to us. It wasn't about people knowing what she did. It was about true love. She loved everyone she met. We have no idea how many people she touched in her life. Mom's obituary was all about facts. What I want to do is to share with you who my mom was to all of us . . . .

At work, I remember her best in the break room, putting together the sports pools and parties, and counseling coworkers, but the fact is she still did her job and more. You don't last that many years without being a valuable employee, but she made us believe it was fun.

No matter how tired she was after work, she came home with a smile on her face, did chores, took us to ballgames, then fixed each of us what we wanted for dinner. Liver for dad, hot dog for me, meat loaf for Kirk, chicken for Craig, and Chris, well, he was the baby. She took him out for dinner.

Come 11:00 or 12:00 at night, she would finally lay down on the couch and say, "I am just resting my eyes." We didn't want her to go to sleep yet, because she was so much fun. This wasn't just one day, but every day . . . .

My mom loved sports. She was always supportive of our efforts in any sport. When Kirk was about twenty, he coached Little League.

He and his other coach were thrown out of the game. Imagine that. When the umpire said, "You will have to forfeit," Mom said, "Oh no, they don't," and became the first female coach in our Little League. It didn't matter what happened in our lives, whether it was sports, school, or sickness, she was always our coach. She wanted us to do our best, play to win, and lose with dignity . . . .

They say life is a gamble and no one practiced that more than my mom did. My mom loved betting pools. It didn't matter if it was sports or the birth date of an expected grandchild . . . .

When I was young, I would wait at my mom's office for her to take me to my doctors' appointments. I always knew she worked with numbers, but I didn't realize, until I was about fifteen, she was in accounting and not a bookie. To my mom, gambling was not about money. Whether it was a family reunion or casino night at the church, it was about fun and bringing all ages together.

Whatever mom did, she did to the fullest.

She didn't just go to church, she lived it. She was on the council; she ran bingo, made dinners, and, again, created the church pool.

She didn't just go watch her grandkids play sports, she brought her cowbell and rang it loudly and frequently. She cheered louder than anyone and bought treats for all the kids after the game . . . .

Mom didn't just go visit a sick friend; she would go regularly, as well as take a meal and clean their house at the same time . . . .

My mom and dad met in grade school, began going together in high school, and celebrated their fiftieth wedding anniversary last year. Her deep love for my dad was evident throughout our growing-up years and to the very end. My dad's love for her was a sustaining force, especially throughout this past year, when he remained at her side until the very end. What an example for us all.

As I approached the end of the talk, my emotions were hard to contain and the words became more difficult to say. Although still outwardly composed, I kept my face down as I finished.

The greatest gift from Mom was her deep devotion to God. She taught us to always trust in God, pray to Him, and He will lead us down the right path.

Mom loved life and, to her, it was simple. It was love of God and family and friends. Everyone who met my mom was touched by her. We will all miss her greatly, but this is not a sad time. Today is a day of celebration of a life well-lived, a life loved and experienced to the fullest.

You played the game, Mom. You reached the final round, and you won the trophy.

I then raised Mom's cowbell, and shook it, one last time, as I left the lectern. All my emotions erupted as I went out the side door, tears streaming down my cheeks. Father John and Father Vincent immediately started applauding. Megan followed me outside, to make sure I was all right.

The greatest compliment I received was from my nine-year-old nephew Davis, who told his dad after the funeral, as they were on their way to the cemetery, "That Uncle Ward is funny." If Davis remembers his Grandma's funeral as being somewhat funny, my mother will be proud, and happy.

SIGNS OF PRESENCE

Mom had told Mary Kay and Chris a couple of weeks before she died, that she had worried about me so much since the day I was born. (Mom used to tell me she prayed to St. Jude for me. "How nice," I thought—until I realized he is the patron saint of hopeless cases.)

Now she told them that I was the one she worried about least. Knowing my brothers, I understood why. But this was a great compliment to my growth and my faith in God, His love for me, and, in my mind, a tribute to Mom and Dad.

The night following my mother's funeral, I had a beautiful dream. I was standing in the backyard of the house I grew up in. I looked into the window, and saw Mom inside, looking out at me, smiling and waving.

When I awoke, I felt so peaceful and had enjoyed seeing Mom. Later that day, I shared the dream with Donna, and said, "I loved seeing Mom, but I miss her voice. I wish I could have talked to her, or at least heard her voice."

The next night, I had another dream. I was at my aunt's house, the phone rang, and my aunt said, "Ward, the phone is for you."

After saying hello, I heard my mom laughing, and then she said, "Hello, it's me, and you'll always remember my voice." Those were two of the most peaceful and enjoyable dreams I have ever had.

But there were many other signs, too, of Mom's presence in the time following her death. All brought peace, comfort, and warmth to those who experienced them.

On Friday, the day following Mom's funeral, Chris and Carrie and their children drove back to California.

Over the previous several months, five-year-old Tana, their youngest, had been sick with numerous headaches. After many tests, doctors were still unable to find the cause, so more extensive tests had been arranged for their return from Kansas. No one had told my mother about her grandchild's problem, not wanting to worry her.

Chris's family arrived home Sunday evening, just in time for Tana's tests early Monday morning.

When Carrie and Tana arrived at the doctor's office bright and early that Monday, the nurse asked why they had come.

"Tana has been scheduled for some tests," Carrie replied.

The nurse then said, "I called your home last Friday to confirm the tests and a lady answered the phone. She said she was Tana's grandma, that Tana was fine, and didn't need any tests done. I told her thanks, and we cancelled the tests."

"Last Thursday was Grandma's funeral in Kansas, and no one was at our house," Carrie said.

The nurse had chills up her spine as she repeated, "A grandma answered the phone and told me Tana was fine."

And she was, and still is.

The same week, Chris and Carrie's oldest, eleven-year-old Ryan, went to a swimming birthday party for a friend. The parents of the birthday boy bought a different kind of beach ball for each of the more than thirty children who attended. The beach ball with Ryan's name on it was yellow, and featured a smiley face—just like the hospital balloon.

Davis woke up one morning and told his mom he had had a dream. At first he said he didn't want to talk about it, but Carrie finally convinced him to share it with her.

"I had a dream about Grandma," he said. "I didn't want her to talk, so she handed me a note that said the oldest boy was going to have a surprise."

Neither Carrie or Davis knew who was meant by "the oldest boy." But, a few days later, Carrie got a call. My brother Kirk—the oldest boy in our family—said, "I have a surprise. My daughter Megan just had her baby, and it's a girl!" This healthy little girl was named Kylie Jo after my mother, Joan, and would have been her first great-grandchild.

Chris and Carrie's seven-year-old son, Matthew, was in his first week of school the fall after my mother's death when his teacher from the previous year found him.

"Matthew," she said, "when you were in Kansas, at the end of the school year, our class had a pottery day. Since you were taking care of your grandma, I decorated some pottery for you."

"Thank you," Matthew said. The pottery was decorated with yellow smiley faces.

While driving to work one afternoon, Carrie began missing Mom and became teary-eyed as a song played at the funeral came on the radio. Carrie glanced in her rearview mirror and saw an air freshener hanging from another car's mirror—a yellow, smiley face, air freshener.

When she pulled up to her destination and got out of the car, she noticed two big, yellow, smiley face balloons in the sky.

A Norton friend was on her way to Kearney, Nebraska. As she drove, Jenny was sharing all the stories of the smiley face balloon with her daughter, Erin. Erin was having a hard time believing these stories, when, suddenly, hanging on a clothesline in the backyard of a house they were passing, was a huge, yellow, smiley face rug. "Whoa," Erin said, and needed no more proof. They had never seen that rug before, and have never seen it since.

Aunt Nadyne, my mom's sister and best friend, had a weed in her front yard that she had intended, for more than a year, to pull out of the ground, but had never got around to doing so. Within a few days of my mother's death, that weed turned into a sunflower, my mom's favorite Kansas flower.

A week after my mom's death, Nadyne received smiley face stamps in the mail. She was a devout Catholic, but never one to talk about spiritual things—until these two occurrences.

A couple of weeks later, my aunt, her son Patrick, Annie, and I were sitting in Nadyne's kitchen, talking about spiritual happenings, when a cross suddenly appeared on the back of a picture Patrick was holding. We passed the picture around and each of us was awed by what we were seeing. The bright white cross was even lighter than the white on the back of the picture.

After sharing even more stories that night, we were astonished to see the cross disappear as fast as it had come.

Marlene, a friend of my mother's since childhood, was helping console a friend whose wife had just died. Marlene shared her faith and belief in God, telling stories about close friends who had passed away.

She told me later, "For some reason, I focused mostly on stories about Joan, and tears began to flow for me and for Joan." Just then Marlene's father shouted from the kitchen, "Look out your window. The wind is blowing terribly!"

Marlene walked to the window and saw a yellow, smiley face balloon in her yard. "The wind should have blown it away immediately," she told me. "But I saw it, I watched it, and then it went up and blew into the heavens, east."

Coincidences or miracles? A friend once told me a coincidence is God remaining anonymous. I find no need to convince anyone of anything. I just thank God for giving us comfort and peace through these signs. They were a gift and a reminder God is always with us, whether we acknowledge His presence or not.

An acquaintance once sarcastically said to me, "You just look and see God in *every little thing.*"

I paused, thought for a moment, and said, with an upbeat voice, "That's right. I do!"

REWARDS

"You just look and see God in *every little thing*," was a great compliment. Even though the comment was sarcastic, it meant someone had noticed the way I was trying to live.

Frankly, my growth was surprising even to me. I *was* seeing God more than ever. My parents always told me to look for the good in things and now I truly was. I was looking for the good—and the God—in all things, even in the devastating loss of my mother. I was now able to see how God was carrying me through, strengthening my faith, bringing me peace, and filling me with His love. In fact, without my knowing it, God had helped prepare me for my own mother's death by leading me to hospice and those special patients with whom I'd worked.

I was learning, understanding, and truly walking with God. (Or, in my case, I was limping with the Lord.) God's love continued to fill my soul and every part of my life.

ANOTHER ANSWERED PRAYER

Most of the time I sit in church, praying, listening, and reflecting, I am alone, but, on occasion, the church secretary stops in to practice playing the piano. One afternoon, with the peaceful sounds of Jani's music in the background, I asked God for prayers to say for the dying. I love using my own words in prayer, but I also love prayers I was taught as a child, such as the rosary. I wanted prayers to meditate on when I sat alone with a dying patient. So I asked.

That evening, I began flicking through the TV channels. I came across EWTN, a Roman Catholic network I'd never watched before. This time, my attention was caught by a program telling the story of Sister Faustina Kowalska. In the middle of the show, I received a hospice call, so had to leave, but I turned on the VCR to be sure I could see the rest of the program.

The next afternoon, I was getting ready to watch the videotape I'd made, when, at about ten minutes until three, I felt a strong urge to go to church, and so I did. I didn't stay long, just enough for a few prayers.

When I arrived home, I returned to the story of Sister Faustina, a nun who became a saint because of her relationship with Jesus. She was the one to whom Jesus gave the Chaplet of Divine Mercy, a set of prayers for the dying, meant—to my surprise—to be prayed every day at 3:00 P.M.

God never ceases to amaze me. My prayer for help was answered so quickly, and even more astonishing was my urge to head to the church at three o'clock, before I knew anything about these prayers and the time they were meant to be said.

HUGS AND HUMOR

From the biggest of things to the smallest, I was not only feeling, but also seeing, God's love everywhere. Especially in others.

Following a speech one evening, many people approached me with words of support and appreciation. I was especially touched when a mentally disabled gentleman, who I am not even sure was able to understand my message, gave me the most beautiful hug.

Nearing the end of another talk, I said, "It's been a long time since I got a standing ovation, so, before I finish, would you all please stand?" They all laughed. I received one of the nicest compliments ever when, during the question-and-answer period, a lovely young woman named Kendra said, "I hope when I am dying, you will come sit next to me and tell stories." Later, as I left, the audience again stood and applauded. (My lesson is, if you ever need a standing ovation, just ask. Or a hug, or an ear, or a shoulder.)

When things are going really well and I get a little too proud of myself, God also lets me know that. A friend's twelve-year-old daughter, Courtney, asked me to speak at her church, and I was happy to fulfill her request. I took Pam and her friend Amanda with me for this speech to an audience mostly of children. I told stories about my life and talked about being happy, looking for the good in everything, accepting yourself, and being proud when you look in the mirror. "Happiness is a choice," I said. During the question-and-answer period, Pam (who has a wonderful sense of humor) raised her hand and said, "Dad, you're not always happy. I have seen you grumpy with me plenty of times." Everyone laughed, and so did I.

On another occasion, I was speaking at a Mother's Day dinner to a group of women of all ages, including a few children. Before I spoke, a little first-grade girl asked if I was the speaker.

"Yes," I said. "I will try to be funny and not talk long."

"Okay," she said, smiling.

After I finished, I was visiting with a few older ladies, while this beautiful little girl stood silently and patiently, waiting to talk with me. An after-dinner mint I had saved to eat following my speech, was also waiting at my place at the table.

When it was her turn, this little girl said, "You were funny, and did you really fall in a fryer?"

"Yes," I said, "and thank you." I was feeling proud that I had reached all ages through my speech, especially that I had made a huge impact on this little girl. She then pointed her finger toward the table and asked, "Is that mint spoken for?"

ANOTHER HARD GOODBYE

Just months following my mother's death, Aunt Nadyne became deathly ill. Her sisters Dorothy and Patsy, my brother Craig and I, all of her children, and many of her grandchildren, traveled from throughout the country to be with her in the hospital during her last hours. Sad, and uneasy with her illness, we all talked quietly in her room, held hands, and said the Lord's Prayer.

As time wore on, I noticed her family just staring at her, silently. No one knew what to say or do. The room was so quiet; the only sounds were the monitors and Aunt Nadyne's shallow breathing. Because of my hospice experiences, I knew her time to move on was coming soon. I suggested everyone say their goodbyes, thank her, and let her know they'd be all right.

When everyone had done so, we began reminiscing about our childhoods and sharing stories that made us laugh. While we laughed, Aunt Nadyne died and went home to God. With her great sense of humor, what more beautiful time for her to leave than with our laughter in the background.

When someone is terminal, whether a hospice patient or a family member, it is always difficult and sad when they die. But it is also a relief, as our loved ones will no longer have to suffer.

Months earlier, while our mother lay dying in the hospital, Chris and I sat in the lobby talking, and wondering why Mom had to die. During our conversation, Chris said, "Mom has always tried to help so many people. Maybe one reason for her death is she will be helping others cross over. If someone special to her dies soon after her death, this will make more sense to me."

Nadyne was my Mom's closest sister. She was the godmother to two of my brothers. My mom always tried to take care of her. Within months of my mother's death, Aunt Nadyne died peacefully. I believe Mom was waiting to help her, one last time.

A VOLUNTEER FOR HOSPICE

A few weeks after my aunt's death, I entered the hospital room of an eighty-eight-year-old woman and introduced myself as a volunteer for hospice. The patient smiled and said, "I guess I am a volunteer for hospice as well." I laughed and we began getting to know one another.

During another visit, the woman asked, "Who is that standing behind you?"

Knowing I was the only other person in the room (although I did peek over my shoulder), I answered with a question: "Is it an angel?"

The patient said, "Well, angels need to do good for God also."

We became good friends over the next several weeks. I loved her smile and her sense of humor. One afternoon, I said I wished the hospital windows were lower so she could see outside from her bed, and enjoy the beautiful view. She responded, "That would be nice, but it would be nicer if I could just see."

On another occasion, one of my favorite nurses walked in. Rikki asked the patient, "How do you like Ward?"

"Wonderful. I just wish I'd met him sixty years ago!" Once again, this lovely woman had so much peace as she approached death, that she brought laughter, joy, and love into my life. The rewards of hospice work are endless.

HELP FOR FAMILIES

Hospice workers learn early that the families of patients are just as important as the patients.

Late one evening, my cell phone began ringing. As I answered, I noticed the time was 11:11 P.M., and instantly thought of God's love. Ever since the minister had told me, when my mom was dying, about seeing ones, they seemed to show up everywhere. Just another example of how, while trying to become closer to God, I was being reminded of Him in so many different and simple ways. I was ready for anything as I said hello.

"Please come to the hospital. My grandma is dying," said a scared young man. I'd never met the young man, in his late teens, but he was the grandson of my hospice patient. I immediately headed to the hospital.

Many family members and both Betty and I stood around the patient's bed, hoping and praying her death would be peaceful. After a couple of hours, however, I was getting tired and felt the need to go home and rest. But I also wanted to "be there" for the family. I prayed silently, "Lord, what else do I need to do before I leave?"

Within two minutes of my asking the question, God answered. I left to go to the restroom and found the grandson who had called me, standing alone outside the room, upset and sad. This young man had never lost anyone close and was obviously scared, and full of emotions. We began talking, becoming instant friends, and sat in the lobby, sharing conversation and feelings for a half-hour, until 2:00 A.M.

I was now extremely tired, and, though the patient was getting close to death, I didn't feel the need to stay with the family during the dying process.

When Donna's father, Richard, had been dying, we stayed with him continually, but he didn't die until I left. I had always wanted to be with my mother when she died, but knew that also wasn't meant to be. Families can take turns sitting with a dying patient constantly, and, in the five minutes no one is in the room, the patient will die. Many of us want certain things to go certain ways, but, whether we are nearing the moment of death for a hospice patient or a family member, we must trust in God. We must remember it is God's will and His time. We die alone with God, whether we are surrounded by family and friends or totally by ourselves.

I knew the family would be in good hands with Betty. So, exhausted and feeling the most important part of my job was over, I left for home as the young man headed back into the room. Within minutes of my leaving, the patient died peacefully, with her loving family surrounding her bedside.

ANOTHER BELL

One summer afternoon, I met a new hospice patient, a man in his early sixties, dying of cancer. Ron and I were visiting on his front porch when I asked if there was anything I could get him to eat or drink. He said, "No thanks. If I need something, I just ring my cowbell." He held up a bell, then shook it loudly. I laughed and, of course, thought of my late mother and her ringing her cowbell at all the grandkids' sporting events. I then realized it was July 7, the first anniversary of my mother's death. I felt as if my mother were saying hello, reminding me she had died on this day, and telling me how proud she was of my hospice work.

During another visit on a hot afternoon, Ron asked if I would go to the store and get him some ice cream. Many times hospice patients (like most of us) don't like to ask for help with anything. So, though I was really tired and wanted to go home and take a nap, I was pleased to run an errand for him. When I returned, Ron insisted on me staying and eating a bowl of ice cream with him. I was happy to oblige, as I haven't yet found any ice cream I didn't like.

I was also happy to be his guest, for it is very important to let hospice patients give to us, even something as small as a bowl of ice cream. Dying people typically suffer a devastating loss of independence. Permitting them to do things for others, when they can, helps them feel productive again. After all, hospice volunteers and all of us who love to help, do so for the joys of giving. We must always allow others to enjoy that feeling, too.

Several weeks and many visits later, Ron's health had declined. Kerri, a young woman now taking care of the man who had raised her, called. "Ron is getting close to death," she said. "Can you please come over soon? You are our spiritual guy and we could use your help."

"I'm on my way," I said.

When I arrived, I found everyone in Ron's bedroom—and couldn't think of a thing to say. I thought, "Oh great. Some really good spiritual guy you are, who can't think of anything to say," despite knowing that sometimes the best thing said is nothing at all.

After long minutes of silence, I asked if they would like to pray together. All the children thought that would be nice, so we held hands and said the Lord's Prayer. Within fifteen minutes, Ron peacefully passed away.

A few days later, I went to an empty church to sit quietly and pray. Walking toward the door, I was stopped by a child's voice yelling, "Ward! Ward!"

I looked around, didn't see anything, so continued toward the church until, once again, the voice yelled.

"Ward! Over here, Ward."

I looked all around and still couldn't see anything. I feel God's guidance daily and, for a moment, chuckling to myself, I thought, "Wow, I am now hearing Jesus using a child's voice."

Finally, the head of a four-year-old boy caught my eye. He was in the backyard of a daycare center across the street, peeking over a fence to which he was hanging on tightly. "Ward!"

This little boy, Dallas, had been like a grandson to Ron.

When I waved back, Dallas yelled, "This is my friend Levi. He's four, too."

Another head popped up over the fence; now there were two little boys hanging on. Dallas put an arm around his buddy and kept on yelling. "How are you? What are you doing?"

I yelled back to those two four-year-old kids, and we conversed for a couple of minutes. Then I said goodbye and headed into the empty church.

A child remembered me and wanted me to meet his buddy, even though we had met through hospice and the death of a loved one. I always try hard to help everyone involved in the death of someone they care about, and this young boy was truly a gift. I smiled and thanked God as I sat down in a pew. God had truly blessed me. When I asked for prayers for the dying, He sent them. When I gave speeches, I saw God in others and was rewarded by a hug and caring words. And now I had heard a four-year-old yelling my name with excitement.

SIGNS OF HOPE

These days, I was seeing God in nearly everything and everyone, but, most important, in myself. I now had, in my daily life, constant reminders of God's love, of doing His will, of walking with and being thankful to Him. Some were common and simple, things I had chosen to do, like wearing a wristband that reads, "Jesus I Trust in You," and a necklace with a crucifix. And then there were the uncommon gifts, the smiley faces, seeing ones in a row, and light bulbs going out. They were a true blessing, and they and other signs like them continued to show up without my looking for them.

I once drove more than two hours to do a speech, and talked to God most of the way. I asked God if I was doing well enough in my speeches because it had been a long time since I had received a standing ovation. Following a beautiful dinner, I faced an audience from five-years-old to eighty that filled the room. Forty minutes later, I finished talking and heard God's answer loud and clear as everyone stood and applauded (without me asking).

A couple years after my mother died, Donna and I invited everyone over for Thanksgiving dinner, and nearly all our relatives in Norton showed up. We had a wonderful time, and, as I took pictures, I thought how proud my mom would be of us all getting together for the holiday.

A few days later, I was enjoying the newly-developed pictures when I stopped at one, shocked at what I saw. It showed Dad, Jack and Esther, Grandma, Ray and Jean, eating dinner at the kitchen table, but, up in the corner, there was a face watching them—a face that looked just like my mother's.

There was my mom's face, above my dad's shoulder, looking directly at my grandma. I immediately knew this was a gift from God, but still wondered if it could really be her face. I looked again through the other pictures and noticed one with a circle on the wall directly above an angel figurine on our mantle. In the circle was a smiley face, just like the one on Mom's "angel balloon."

I showed the first picture to Megan and to my Dad at separate times without saying anything to either one. Megan got goose bumps, and said, "It's Grandma Joan." When I showed Dad the picture, he first looked shocked, but then smiled. His eyes teared up and he softly said, "Joan."

I shared this picture with several friends, including some ministers. One said, "What a blessing." Another said, "Ward, just keep doing what you're doing."

Annie was next. When she saw the picture, she said, "It's Aunt Joan," and then jokingly added, "I'm glad I'm not in that picture, because one of them may be dying soon." Even though we both laughed, part of me wondered if Annie could be right.

Within three weeks, my one-hundred-year-old grandmother was in the hospital. Grandma's body was beginning to shut down. A century of life was coming to an end.

The next Sunday morning, I slipped and fell while putting on my sock, hurting my foot. I figured if my foot still hurt on Monday, I would see a doctor. Later, I went to the hospital to visit Grandma and, by then, could hardly walk. As I entered her room, I also encountered my dad, Aunt Jody, Aunt Mary Kay, and Dr. Maurer, all wondering what had happened to me.

"I hadn't realized putting on socks was so dangerous," I said.

I decided that seeing Dr. Maurer might be a sign. What with that and barely being able to walk, I asked to have an x-ray. I was immediately put in a wheelchair and escorted to the emergency room.

The nurse asked me numerous questions and began taking my blood pressure, and I suddenly realized this was the first time something like this had happened to me since my mom had died. Mom had always been with me during my surgeries and throughout my life, especially when I was ill or hurt. I truly missed her and, especially, while in the emergency room.

Just then the nurse finished taking my blood pressure. It was 111/77. There were those ones again and also two sevens. My mother had died on July 7—7/7. Once again I felt as if my mother were saying hello and reminding me that she was still with me.

Coincidence? Or was I just looking for something to help me through a tough time? Or was God actually speaking to me? I'll just thank God for giving me strength.

The x-ray showed I had broken my foot. While sitting in the wheelchair, waiting to be released from the emergency room, I bent over to grab my shoe and the chair's back wheels lifted off the ground. My face was headed directly toward the floor, and the sharp corner of the bed. Somehow, when I jerked up, the chair safely sat back on the floor. When I could breathe again, I started laughing and told myself to sit still and not move.

On December 14, twenty years to the day after her husband's death, Grandma passed away. Death is always hard for families and friends, but it's a little easier when someone has had one hundred years of a beautiful life. She was as classy as they come, smart, and the very definition of a "lady."

THE KINDNESS OF STRANGERS

As a child, I had used crutches as well as anyone, but now I learned quickly that, older and weaker, that was not going to be the way for me to get around. I fell three more times that first day and, thankfully, did not break anything else. But I was bruised and sore, and breathing was difficult because my chest hurt so much. Dr. Maurer let me use a boot-type cast and ordered me to stay off my foot.

Soon, however, I was tired of being cooped up in the house and found myself wanting to get outside, even just for a minute.

Despite the fact that it had snowed a few inches the night before and was bitter cold, causing the streets to be extremely icy, I drove to the post office to check the mail. After almost slipping several times while walking up the steps, I realized I had made a big mistake and should not have gotten out of the car.

I checked the mail, said some prayers, and hoped I wouldn't fall as I walked down the steps toward my car. An average-sized gentleman in his sixties very politely said, "Be careful. It's icy."

"I will," I promised.

With my freezing hands barely able to grip the handrail, I went very slowly, and kept quietly asking God to help me.

Several minutes later, I finally arrived at my car. When I opened the door and turned to get in, I saw the gentleman who had told me to be careful standing directly behind me. He had followed one step back of me all the way, to catch me if I fell. What a beautiful gesture. He never said a word that might embarrass me, or even asked if I needed help; he simply quietly performed a very loving and caring act. This was the same place where the woman had once called me a cripple, and I couldn't help recognizing the difference between insensitivity and compassion.

When I started the engine, I glanced at the clock. It was 1:11. So many times before or after spiritual things have taken place, I have seen those ones, and am always reminded to thank God.

One time those ones even showed up for Donna. She and Pam went shopping for the day and found some clothes she liked. Donna had several items in her hand when she said to the cashier, "I'm not sure if I can afford to buy all these clothes. Will you please ring them up and tell me the total?"

The cashier did so and then announced, "The total would be $111."

Donna excitedly said, "Oh, $111! I'll take them all!"

When Donna saw those ones, she thought, "Ward will understand, as his mom and God wanted me to buy them all." (Or maybe Donna just kept adding clothes until she got to $111.)

A few weeks later, following the funeral of a hospice patient, his grown children and I sat in their living room sharing stories of the patient's life.

Unsure why, but feeling I should, I began telling the story about the light bulbs going out after my friend Glenn's death. The family loved the story, but I still didn't know why I brought it up. And so I asked God in prayer as I drove home. When I walked into my house less than five minutes later, the phone was ringing.

I answered, and the daughter of my hospice patient said, "Ward, you'll never guess what happened. We went out to sit on the porch as soon as you left, and the streetlight went out."

Some people never have gone to church. Some people have lost all their faith. Some people feel God has abandoned or hurt them. Some people have never had any hope, or have lost what they did have. The Bible would probably be the last book these people would want to read. So how does God reach them? How do we help them? We help through love and understanding, through example and acceptance, and some-times through stories about light bulbs. I trust in God to guide me. God is all-powerful, all-knowing, and all-loving. He is the One who can.

After sharing many spiritual stories one evening with my friends Re-nee and Eric, I decided to show them the Thanksgiving picture in which my mother's face appeared. They were amazed. Renee asked if I would call and talk to their friend Misty, a mother whose five-year-old son, Jar-ren, had died when he was run over by a fire truck.

I was nervous about calling Misty because I couldn't even imagine losing a child. However, a few months earlier I had been blessed to talk to, and become friends with, Judy Collier, author of *Quit Kissing My Ashes*, a book about the loss of her child. Because of our mutual spiritual experi-ences, Judy and I had connected immediately. Judy, in a small way, had helped me understand the tragedy of her loss, and, more important, the pain she endures daily. I thank God I do not understand what it is to lose a child, but I did learn that I can always be a friend. I can always "be there" to listen to others who have experienced this horrible nightmare.

I prayed for God's guidance and support as I dialed Misty's phone number. No one answered, so I left a message. When I hung up the phone, I noticed I had talked for one minutes and eleven seconds—1:11. Then I picked up the phone to tell Judy about Misty, for I knew Judy would understand Misty's pain far better than I could. Judy's publishing company is named after her late son's favorite number, 42. Judy didn't answer the phone either and so I left another message and hung up. This time I had talked exactly 42 seconds.

God can speak to us in many ways, but the most obvious is through love. Believing that whenever we do something out of love, it is never wrong, I knew my compassion and love for Misty would bring her at least some comfort.

When Misty and I did talk on the phone later that evening, I told her about my life and faith, and how God has guided me through troubles. I shared many of my spiritual experiences, from the lady in white to the smiley face balloon, from the angel on Annie's wall to the stories of lights going out. Near the end of our conversation, I emphatically told Misty, "Keep your eyes open because, during the next couple of days, you will see a smiley face balloon or a light going out." I didn't even realize what I had said until I'd said it. I had never told anyone else with such conviction and surety that something like this would happen, but I felt strongly that God would send her a message to help ease her pain.

The following day, I received the nicest e-mail from Misty, thanking me for taking the time with her. At the end of her note, she said, "I just had a light bulb go out this afternoon!! Amazing! Thank you so much!"

God always finds ways to connect and comfort us, giving us all we need when we have trust in Him.

SHARING STORIES

When giving speeches about my life and experiences, I don't talk about lights going out or smiley face balloons. However, once, during the question-and-answer period following a very spiritual and faith-filled speech to a group of grieving widows, a woman said, "I have never shared this with anyone, for obvious reasons, but, when my husband died, every light bulb in our house went out except one. We had an electrician come over the next day, and he said everything was fine, and all I needed was new light bulbs."

I asked, "Did this bring you peace? And what did you think it was when it happened?"

She answered, "Yes, my daughter and I thought it was God and my husband telling us they were with us, and that my husband was all right."

"Then that is what it was," I said. "We do not need to convince anyone of anything. You knew deep in your soul that this was a sign from God, and all we need to do is be thankful."

I then told a couple of quick stories about lights going out. I also shared that a friend had told me one time that she knew I didn't lie, but some of my stories were hard to believe. I had told her, "That's okay; I will pray for you."

Before two weeks were past, my friend was saying to me, "Ward, you won't believe what happened, and please don't tell anyone." Of course, I immediately began taking notes, knowing this was going to be a good story for my new book! She continued, "While I was sitting in church listening to the preacher, I saw an angel behind him. This angel was huge. When I rubbed my eyes, looked away, and then back again, it was still there. This was so calming and beautiful."

I asked, "Did you tell your pastor?"

"No, I didn't want him to get a big head," she said, laughing. "But I will." (Of course, I did get my friend's permission to tell this beautiful story.)

Another woman in the group I had addressed, also spoke up. "I too have had experiences and was afraid to tell anyone, but God comforted me through nature." Rosalie went on, "Following my husband's death, I went outside and two of the most beautiful butterflies I had ever seen flew over to me and landed on my glasses, where they stayed for several minutes. Since then, butterflies seem to show up all the time, and especially when I need comfort. On another occasion, I was missing my husband while on a walk, pulling two of my grandchildren in their wagon. Two butterflies flew up and circled the kids throughout the six blocks we walked. I just knew it was a gift from God, as it brought peace."

Rosalie had another story, too. "My fourteen-year-old grandson was playing shortstop in the state baseball tournament when a huge butterfly began hovering around him and home plate throughout the game. The umpire, batters, and my grandson were constantly trying to shoo it away, but it wouldn't leave. My grandson began wondering if it was a sign that his late grandpa was enjoying the game from above. The last batter hit a high fly ball, directly above my grandson. He tried to disregard the butterfly and focus on catching the ball and winning the game, muttering to himself, 'Don't drop the ball.' He made the catch and, as soon as he did, the large butterfly flew directly into his forehead, as if saying 'Good catch,' and then flew away."

Our conversation had changed dramatically from extreme grief to hope. These stories of experiences that had brought comfort and love to us, now brought the same things to others. And, again, deep in our souls, we all knew what we were experiencing.

My friend and both women that night had been apprehensive about sharing their stories, as I also used to be on occasion, because of what people might think. Why can't we share our stories of faith without being judged? Many times the ridicule of others keeps us quiet. But when we experience God's love, we should be able to shout with joy. We want to share our hope with the world. So many people are eager to tell me their own spiritual stories because of my faith and openness, because they know I won't judge them. All these stories—the ones others tell me and the ones I tell others—lead to one place. To God.

Lights burning out and the appearance of angels, yellow smiley faces, and butterflies can be simple ways to remind us of God's love, a way easily understood. And they just might lead us to the peace that I saw in my friend Glenn, the peace that Jesus greeted so many with, when He said, "Peace be with you."

I've heard people say believing in God is a crutch or a weakness. Crutches and God enabled me to walk, and I have been physically weak my whole life. So if people think I am weak, why should I care? I'll take my weakness and the strength God gives me any day.

If others think I am nuts, naïve, gullible, and not living in the real world, that's all right, too. Most of these people are more sad, angry, and frustrated than they will admit, and seeing them happy or even smile is a rarity. I am glad to live in peace and will keep looking for God in everything. I'll keep trying to love and accept everyone. I'll gladly stay in what some have called my fictitious world, my happy and peaceful world, a world full of signs of hope. Ultimately, I hope these others will see the peace I have earned and want it for themselves.

SAVING THE WORLD

I hadn't done a speech in a few months and felt as if I needed to keep in practice. So, one morning, I asked God. That afternoon, I received several calls and set dates for seven speeches. Incredible! Later, when I told my wife, she said, "The next time you pray for speeches, ask God if you can get paid for one of them."

One call was from a gentleman referred to me by someone who had heard me speak for hospice. He asked if I would do a speech for a number of ministers and other very religious men from northwest Kansas. Always happy to share my story, I accepted.

The evening came, and I sat alone at a table waiting for dinner to begin. Fifty or sixty men arrived and found places, including one distinguished retired farmer who joined me. We chatted throughout dinner, enjoying each other's company. Definitely a strong conservative, he mentioned a nephew he loved who had come home recently to tell his family he was gay. The man was obviously disturbed by this.

Years before, in the early 1980s, in a San Francisco hospital I had had a surgery—and one of my first experiences with an AIDS victim. No family or friends could visit this young man, in a room just down the hall from me. In fact, the doctors and nurses wore what looked like space suits to tend to him. There he was, dying and all alone, and no one could give him a hug or hold his hand. I felt horribly sad, and upset, too, when I heard people say that this served him right. I believe God is of love, not hatred.

I also had a cousin, Steve, die of AIDS, and all he ever was toward me was caring, accepting, supportive, and loving.

A hospice patient of mine, dying of cancer in another county, happened to be gay. His partner showed as much love, support, and compassion for his companion as I had ever seen. As a Christian, I was deeply saddened when I learned that not one person from a church had even picked up the phone to check on the status of these two lonely men in despair. One was dying and the other was losing his best friend, and feeling as if he were dying himself. We call ourselves Christian, we go to church, and we can't help someone in need because of our judgments? How sad.

Another of my hospice patients had a gay son die of AIDS. She had helped her son, and then had volunteered for an AIDS organization for a number of years. Yet she was afraid to tell anyone of this wonderful work because of the ridicule she would receive from others.

I do not care if anyone agrees or disagrees with the practice of homosexuality, but not loving others is wrong, and attacking them is sick.

One of the most important things I learned as I grew up was that people were not better than I was because they were stronger or could run faster. They were not smarter because they looked "normal." We are all equal in God's eyes. God loves a bum, a rich man, a homosexual, a couple celebrating fifty years of marriage, a prisoner, a jailer, a woman who just had an abortion, a foster mother, a Republican, a Democrat, and me, just as much as He loved His son Jesus.

I sat listening to this gentleman vent and share his beliefs about his nephew being gay and began feeling that the main reason I was there that night was to talk with him.

I said, as nicely and politely as I could, "If you believe this is a sin, then that is your belief. We are all sinners and no sin is worse than another." Of course, being raised a Roman Catholic, I knew the difference between mortal and venial sins, but went on, "Loving people who love us is easy. Loving and accepting those we disagree with, or who hurt us, is more difficult, but rewarding in God's eyes."

The greatest thing about this extremely conservative man was that he listened, and he wanted to learn to love his nephew as he had in the past. I continued, "The only difference between yesterday's love and today's love for your nephew is your perception and judgment of him. Even if you feel he is wrong, your love should be what's right."

In the background I heard another gentleman begin my introduction. As I stood, I said, "Listen to my talk tonight and maybe it'll help."

I walked up to the podium and talked about my journey through life, and my faith and acceptance of others as well as myself. Thirty minutes later I finished with, "Thank you and God bless all of you."

All the men stood, applauding. I had shared my faith with those who preached and lived their faith, and I had received a standing ovation.

As I returned to my seat, one man stopped me, shook my hand, thanked me for a wonderful talk, and said, "Ward, when you were born, and throughout your life, you were the less fortunate. Now, your faith is so incredible that it is we who are the less fortunate."

Back at my table, the gentleman with the gay nephew reached over to shake my hand. With tears in his eyes, he said, "Thank you."

Both comments touched my heart, and, once again, I realized how much I had grown since seeing the peace in Glenn. I was now living with God day-to-day, but, whether I was raising the kids, coaching, teaching, or doing hospice, my life was anything but mundane.

HELPING

In all my years of being married to my wonderful wife, I don't ever remember a time when something broke in our house and I have fixed it the same day.

Mainly that's because I can't fix much myself, which means I have to ask for help. We have many friends always willing to help, but, like most people, I hate to ask, even though I know that asking for help can be just as important as helping others. (However, my brother Kirk, whom I ask quite often, has suggested I ought to spread that joy around.)

One Saturday morning as Donna was leaving for work, she told me the toilet had broken. After stopping by the church that afternoon, and while running a few other errands, I decided to pick up the parts for the toilet at the hardware store. As I left the store, my friend Harold was on his way in.

"What did you buy?" he asked.

"Just had to pick up a few parts for the toilet," I said.

Refraining from laughing, he glanced into my bag and said, "I'll be over in ten minutes to fix your toilet."

Not only did Harold fix my toilet in fewer than five minutes, but he had to exchange all the parts I had bought because they were the wrong ones. When Donna arrived home and used the restroom, it was lucky she was sitting down because, when she noticed the toilet had been fixed, she nearly fainted.

There are so many loving, caring, giving people in the world, helping others, despite the fact that we mostly hear about the ones who aren't.

My life could be compared to an hourglass. So many people gave to me; now I was trying to give to others. When you are walking with God, you are rewarded by giving.

As summer approached, two friends who run the Norton Recreation Center asked me to coach a baseball team. "The thirteen- to fifteen-year-old kids won't be able to play if they don't have a coach," Steve and Joan told me.

I was nervous about taking this on, remembering how sick I had gotten the last time I tried to coach. However, many parents said they would help, especially with the physical parts of coaching, and so I decided I would try. I would continue doing hospice, but looked forward to adding a focus on youth to my work with the dying, all while still helping others.

During the first practice, I hit a few ground balls and threw the ball about five times. I knew I shouldn't have, but I wanted to try. Unfortunately, for the next three days, I could barely lift my arms. So playing catch or hitting balls was out of the question.

Nevertheless, coaching and being around these young people was a lot of fun, and I seemed to laugh more than ever. During one game, I continued moving a particular player to different positions. In every one, he dropped fly balls. As I walked by this boy's father later in the game, he encouraged me and jokingly said, "You're going to have a hard time finding a place for him to play."

In another game, a different player missed a fly ball. When the other team laughed, he casually flipped them the bird. I tried hard not to laugh as I immediately called a time-out and took him out of the game. When he came off the field and into the dugout, I asked him, "Why did I take you out of the game?"

"Because I missed the ball."

"No," I said. "You can't flip the other team off." When people treat us poorly, we should not immediately react with negativity.

I am as competitive and determined to win as anyone. But learning and improving, having fun and being good sports, were my most important lessons in coaching the game.

We lost more games than we won, and some were by ways I had never before seen. For example, one time our pitcher struck out *six* batters in one inning. Not only that, but he didn't give up a single hit, yet the other team scored six runs. You see, our catcher had a hard time holding onto the ball on the third strike, allowing the batters to reach first base.

Although we struggled, I was truly enjoying the personalities of all the kids. We did improve throughout the year and actually became a pretty good team by tournament time. In fact, we came within one out of making it to the regional playoffs.

Physically, I had a tough time with fatigue and the usual aches and pains, but, with the help and support of the parents, I sure had a lot of fun.

MORE TIME WITH KIDS...

Following the baseball season, my church's religious education coordinator asked if I would teach CCD—Sunday School for the eighth-graders. Having finished baseball and enjoying being around young people, I said, "Sure."

During our first class, I told the students, if they never missed a session, I would give them twenty dollars worth of gifts at the end of year. If they did miss a class, they could volunteer for an hour to make it up. (Bribery always worked well with me when I was a child.) When I told

Donna about this, she asked, "Twenty bucks? Where are you going to get the twenty dollars for each kid?"

"God will provide," I said.

I try very hard to make class fun and enjoyable. If the kids look forward to coming, I feel they learn more.

Four different parents came up to me the next day to tell me how much their children had enjoyed the class. One student, Conner, told his dad, Dan, all about the class and the presents I said I would give them. Dan told me later that he wanted to help with money for the presents. God always does provide, and Dan was another of His blessings (especially financially, for Donna).

I also told my students they could invite any of their friends to our class. The following session, a few kids did bring friends from other churches. I began by talking about God and the different religions. I told the kids how happy I was that some of them had brought their friends to the only church where God really was. Familiar with my sense of humor, everyone laughed—except one of the guests. I immediately told them I was kidding, and that God was in all churches. Although this began as a joke, it gave me the opportunity to remind the kids that many people in this world will judge you, and like you or not, by the color of your skin, the way you look, your job, and even the church in which you worship. And that is never of God.

One evening, during a discussion of prayer, I asked the students if they prayed every day. Only a few raised their hands. I then asked, "Well, when do you pray?"

Many kids said, all at once, "When I am in trouble . . . when I need help."

"Just like most of us adults," I responded. "And then we wonder why God allows bad things to happen."

The kids loved hearing stories of my daily life and how I lived trying to listen to and follow God's will. One time I asked them why they thought so many "God things" happened to me. As we went around the room, I was stunned at their answers. One said, "You opened up and allowed God to come in," and, "You're on the right path." Another said, "After all the things you've been through, you still trust Jesus," and "You look for

Him in all things." Some other comments were, "You read the Bible . . . you follow God's guidance . . . you're faithful . . . you pray a lot."

Simple yet profound answers from eighth-grade kids who obviously understood both me and how to live a faith-filled life. Deep in our souls, most of us know these answers and how we should live.

. . . AND THE ELDERLY

I stopped by the nursing home to visit some residents one Sunday evening. These visits began when a woman heard me praying with a hospice patient there, and asked me to pray with her, too. I then met other residents who enjoyed having visitors.

When I entered the room of a nice lady I had visited several times, she was agitated. I asked what was wrong, and she told me they had had a church service that day that was terrible. "The preacher was a fill-in and he didn't dress very well," she said. Then she looked directly at me and said, "The preacher dressed terrible, but not as bad as you." I wanted to laugh but held back and continued to listen. She went on to describe how the music and prayers weren't very good either.

When she finally finished, I said, "Well, I know God hears our prayers no matter how badly we pray. And music is beautiful to His ears no matter how badly we sing." Then I added, "As far as my clothes, I cannot put on a tie without help. My clothes are simply the easiest for me to wear. Judging others by their appearance is wrong. We may not know why people dress the way they do, but the man did come, and he did the best he could so all of you could have church."

She understood, and began looking at the positive. By the time I left, she was thankful for having had church and for my visit. I then went into the room of another resident, a lady in her nineties. "How are you today?" I asked.

She softly said, "Fine," but continued, "We had church today and I played the music on the piano. I haven't played for years because of my arthritis, but I wanted to try. No one seemed to enjoy my music."

I felt so sad for her, knowing all we can do is our best, and I reminded her, too, that God always hears her music as beautiful.

After I got home, Donna asked, "How do you know what to say?

What do you talk about with the residents?"

"All I have to do is ask questions and they will talk," I said. "I probably enjoy the visits more than the residents do. After all, we have a lot in common, especially our aches and pains." Many nursing home residents just want a friend, or someone to talk with occasionally. Sometimes I just watch television or sit quietly with them. We all want the same thing—we all want to feel important. No one wants to be lonely. And we can all help others, even though we can't all visit the elderly, or teach Sunday School, or work with the dying. I am doing what I feel God is calling me to do. Many people would have a hard time giving a speech or doing hospice work. Am I better than they are? Obviously not. We are all called for different reasons and on different journeys, but everyone can affect people in their daily lives. The littlest things in life are often the most important.

When I was younger, I felt I needed to "save the world." Some of that came from my own feelings, and some from the way I was treated. I wanted to do wonderful things in order to be the equal of others. Now I have learned we can all "save the world" in our own little environments.

By raising two kids and living my life for God, I can make a difference. The people we meet every day can be affected by a smile. Children can be affected by our example. Every person in our life can be affected by our love—our unconditional love.

GOD THINGS

God talks to each of us in many different ways throughout the day. We only have to look and listen. When I pray for God's guidance and direction, I must truly pay attention. Seeing, listening to, and trusting in God, no matter how good or bad things are, continue to become easier as my faith grows.

A perfect example of this is the sequence of events on one single day, a day that began with an early morning trip to the post office to mail a stack of payments for bills.

While I was checking my box for mail, a gentleman tapped me on the shoulder and asked, "Are you Ward?"

"Yes," I answered.

"What a God thing! My mother died recently and yesterday someone told me to get in touch with you. And here you are."

We talked for several minutes and I gave him my phone number with an invitation to call me anytime. I then realized I had left my outgoing mail in the car. "Oh well," I thought. "I'm too tired to walk down the steps and back; I'll mail it tomorrow instead."

I left the post office and headed to the Endzone sporting goods store to pay another bill. I handed Shauna the payment and left. As I was getting into my car, Shauna ran outside after me, yelling, "Ward, this check is made out to Nex-Tech."

That's how I learned I had put all the checks into the wrong envelopes. This would have been just an inconvenience, but, while living with my focus on God, it was an inconvenience I thanked Him for saving me from. And, even if I had mailed all those incorrect payments, I still would have felt He clearly wanted me somewhere else, and not been too frustrated.

A little while later, still running errands, I felt a strong desire to stop at the florist's and send a plant to a resident at the nursing home. I very seldom send flowers to anyone except my wife, and that happens only every few years, so this was out of the ordinary. But I felt strongly God wanted me to send them, and I did.

I then went to church to sit alone and pray for awhile. Even when I have nothing particular to pray about, I love sitting there quietly; it always helps me relax and focus on His guidance.

Getting tired and needing a nap, I started for home, but made one more stop, at United Northwest Credit Union. When I talk to young people, I often remind them of the importance of choosing to be happy, and of how something as simple as a smile can make someone's day, as well as your own. Well, the employees of this credit union practice what I preach. Each one always has a kind word for me. Isn't it sad that this is such a rarity in today's society that I even notice? But, though I barely have enough money even to have an account, they still treat me like a million bucks.

When I woke from my nap, I felt a strong urge to go to church again. Twice in one is day is unusual for me, but I trusted in His guidance.

On my way to church, I noticed I was headed in the wrong direction, finding myself for no apparent reason in the left-turn lane at the only stoplight in town. Instead of causing a wreck, I just went left when the light turned green, then decided I might as well stop at the hospital and visit my hospice patient for a few minutes.

Within minutes of entering her room, the phone rang. She was much too weak to answer, and, had I not been there, she would have missed this conversation with her daughter in another state. It turned out to be the last conversation the two ever had.

Eventually I did reach the church. While I was sitting, quietly praying, in walked a friend I hadn't seen for a couple of weeks. She said, "Ward, I haven't been feeling well spiritually . . . been a little bummed. While driving home a different way than usual, I noticed your car out front, so I stopped. Thank God you were here."

She was suffering from cancer and dealing with all the effects of che-motherapy. We talked and filled our souls with the love of God.

Later that evening, when I went to visit the resident to whom I had impulsively sent the plant, she was so appreciative and thankful. She said, "Ward, the plant couldn't have come at a better time. If my husband were still alive, today would have been our seventieth wedding anniversary."

"Incredible," I thought.

On that one ordinary day, I was at the post office at the right time to meet a stranger who needed a friend, I made a wrong turn that put me in the hospital so a mother and daughter could say their goodbyes, I sat alone in church waiting for a friend who just happened to show up after coming home by a different route, and I unknowingly sent a plant to an elderly woman on her wedding anniversary.

These were all just simple little "God things" I did throughout the day by trying to follow His guidance, but, as always, these simple little things can be the most important in our lives. Many times we will not see the results of listening to God, but sometimes we are blessed to do so. Either way, we need to be thankful.

A BREAK

A few days later, I walked in to visit my eighty-eight-year-old hospice patient who immediately said, "Where did they take my mom?"

"I'm not sure," I answered. "Was your mom here visiting?"

"Yes. Did you see her? Will she be back?"

I told her, "No, I didn't see her, but, if she was here earlier, I am sure she'll be back."

Another day this same patient was very restless. Her legs were cold and that was bothering her a great deal. I asked if she would like to pray, and we did. Within a few minutes of finishing our prayers, she said, "Isn't that beautiful how the light comes through the ceiling and shines on my legs? They feel warm and so much better."

"Yes," I said. "God must have answered our prayers." She smiled and rested comfortably the remainder of the evening.

This woman's son-in-law in another state died suddenly, and the family didn't know whether to tell her. They asked me what to do, and I told them either way was fine; it was their decision. They decided not to tell their mother.

Later, while family members were visiting, the patient turned and, apparently looking at no one, said, "Why is my son-in-law standing over there, naked?" No one had told her anything, and yet, at some level, she knew he had died.

Later, one of the woman's daughters asked me why she had said he was naked. I immediately recalled that, during the time my mother was dying, she had looked outside and said, "Look at all those people playing in the park, naked." I had almost started laughing, but then realized my mom was serious.

I believe that both were describing the people as naked because they didn't have the words to describe what they were seeing. Yet, when dying people see things we don't, we seem either to brush it off as confusion, or try too hard to figure it out. I believe the reason this happened in this case was to bring comfort and peace to the family, and so it did.

This wonderful lady died a short time later. While coming home alone after her funeral, I was overcome with emotion. I wanted to cry, and would have, but couldn't because I was driving. I wondered why I was taking this so hard. What was bothering me? Then I realized I had lost two hospice patients that week and a total of three in a month. I was drained and emotionally spent.

This deep sadness reminded me of when my mother died and I wasn't grieving. I was trying to be tough when Missy, hospice social worker, "just happened" to be at the right place at the right time. Missy had recognized my pain, and reminded me that, if I didn't grieve and take care of myself, I wouldn't be able to help anyone else. Missy knew me well and understood that helping others was very important to me. Grieving is something we all need to take seriously; it's an important part of the healing process.

When I got home, I told Donna, "I am done. I will be taking a break from hospice for a few weeks."

DOING MY BEST

The very next afternoon, Amanda called to tell me there was a new hospice patient specifically asking for me. Taking a break from hospice ended that quickly.

Gary, only in his forties, had been a blessing to me earlier as a caring and compassionate nurse for my mother during her illness. He had not only given his love to my mother, but to all our family. Now I knew I needed to postpone my break and help, for it was the least I could do for such a wonderful man. I knew God would see me through. And He did.

At the viewing following Gary's death, one of his relatives asked if I would be attending the funeral the following day in another town. I was extremely tired and did not feel well, so I said, "I will try to, but, if I don't, it's because I am too tired."

The relative didn't really hear me, as he then asked, "You are still planning to speak at the funeral, right?"

"I'll do my best," I answered.

At home, I told Donna, "I just can't go to the funeral; I am too exhausted and weak. But I'll see how I feel in the morning." My brother Craig wanted to go to the funeral as well. Again, I told him it depended on how I felt.

I knew Gary's family really wanted me to attend, but the only way it would be possible would be through God's intervention. I prayed and asked for God's help.

The next morning, I awoke extremely sore and still exhausted. I again told Donna I wasn't going to be able to make it to the funeral. She said, "Just wait until later and then decide."

One hour before we were to leave, I suddenly had a burst of energy, felt better, and decided I could go. I was literally writing my speech as we walked out the door. We made it to the funeral ten minutes early, and the family was happy to see me. I was feeling great and so thankful I was able to make it.

I talked only a few minutes, paying tribute to the love Gary had for everyone, and, especially, for my family during my mother's illness. Gary loved crossword puzzles, so I closed my speech by saying, "I'd like to end with part of a crossword puzzle . . . two across, a four-letter word for love . . . Gary."

On the way home from the funeral, we stopped at a Christian bookstore. There I noticed a bookmark decorated with smiley faces. That made me smile as I thought about my mom. As we left, I wondered if she had been looking over me during my talk. Just then a jeep drove by, its big fog lights covered with yellow smiley faces.

That evening, I called Annie to tell her this wonderful story of God giving me strength throughout the day, and about the smiley faces on the fog lights. During our conversation, we began discussing memories of our mothers. Annie said, whenever she sees ones in a row, she thinks of my mother. I said, "When I see fours in a row, I think of your mother because she died on April 4, or 4/4." Annie then asked if I thought our mothers looked in on us. I answered, "Sure I do. We just have to pay attention." When I hung up the phone, the amount of time we had talked was 11:44. Of course, I had to call her back.

ANOTHER DAY

God's constant presence in every part of our lives was shown by the strength I received to attend the funeral and make it through the day. However, I hardly slept at all that night, and woke up the next morning extremely sore and terribly exhausted. I was so weak, I could barely get off the couch to do anything, even get a drink of water. I was that tired, and completely drained.

This feeling usually comes on quickly, and I never know when it'll come or go. I simply need to rest, and not think too much, because everything is overwhelming.

However, even on days like this, I am blessed. I can still see and hear God when He sends little messages, and messengers, to help ease my struggles.

Having planted myself safely on the couch, I still managed to crack a tooth, splitting it into three pieces. "Great," I thought. "What else can happen?" Then I took a drink of water and felt a sharp pain go through my entire body. Now I needed to make an appointment with my dentist. And I didn't dare ask again, "What else?" I just chewed on the other side of my mouth, pouted, and tried to stay away from everyone.

A few minutes later, the phone rang. My fellow hospice worker Betty said, "Ward, you'll never guess what happened! I saw a lady at an out-of-town meeting, carrying your book. I asked her, 'Do you know Ward Foley?' She said, 'Yes, and I love him. I read his book and it helped me so much.'" Just a bit later, Dad called to say a woman must have had a wrong number because she had left a message for me on his phone recorder. Despite my exhaustion, I went to Dad's, and was rewarded by hearing the most beautiful message from a lady who had been in the audience at one of my speeches.

On my way home from Dad's, I decided to stop at the nursing home for a quick visit with just one of the residents. After I said hello, Isola asked, "Where have you been? It's been so long since I've seen you." It had only been two days, but I was happy she looked forward to seeing me.

Leaving, I noticed the son of another lady I normally visit standing outside. I watched him walk into the facility and toward his mother's room. I hadn't planned on visiting this woman, but decided I would, so I could say hello to him.

When I walked into her room, I was puzzled because her son wasn't there. I sat down and asked her how her son had been. She said, "Fine, but he's in Kansas City for a couple of days." I was stunned and shocked; I knew I had just seen him enter her room. The resident then told me how lonely she had been and how happy she was I had come to visit that day. "Perfect timing," she said. "God's timing," I thought.

So far, God had given me the strength to get out of the house, over to my Dad's, then to the nursing home and into a woman's room on a day she especially needed a visitor. I headed home with a smile. I knew the day wasn't over yet.

I like to give little inexpensive gifts to my hospice patients and their families, so I order angel pins through Jani, our church secretary. The latest order hadn't shown up in several weeks, and I had nearly forgotten about it. When I got home, I noticed I had a phone message. The recorder said, "You have one message, today, at 11:11 A.M." Hearing 11:11, I immediately thought of God and His angels. The message was from Jani: "Ward, your angels are in."

Wow, was this an elaborate message from God? Who knows? But it made me smile, and reminded me again that God is always with me, especially when I am not feeling well.

After a short nap, still very sore and drained, I began opening the mail. There wasn't one bill, so I knew God was truly with me on this day. There was, however, a letter from the Diocese of Salina, a wonderful letter from the bishop. He had written to me, "May the Lord continue to use you to bring faith and hope to those most in need of these precious gifts." I couldn't believe it. This letter couldn't have come at a better time.

A few hours later, the phone rang again, and this time it was Lynne. She said, "Ward, you're always sharing wonderful 'God stories' with me. Now I have one for you. I was over at my friend's house, telling her the stories of the lights going out. All of a sudden, the light in the room went out, and I think it may have scared my friend half to death."

I laughed and Lynne continued, "As I drove home by myself, I started laughing and mumbled, 'Glenn, you were there, weren't you?' And Ward, as soon as I finished the sentence, the streetlight went out!"

This story Lynne shared with me was wonderful, but what was the message? What did it all mean? Who cares? The fact is God had a wonderful friend call me when I needed it most, another example of the way He works and comforts us through the love of our friends.

A little while later, another friend called to say hi and see how I'd been. "You've just been on my mind today, and I wanted to call," Deb said.

Still having trouble sleeping, I wasn't awakened by the phone ringing again at 12:30 A.M. When I answered, a laughing Annie yelled, "Wardie, God told me you'd be awake! And, boy, do I have a story for you!" All of Annie's stories are wonderful, but this phone call was especially important because it was yet another simple gesture from a caring friend.

None of my friends had known I wasn't feeling well, but all made me feel better. Telephone calls and messages, a special letter, friendly conversations—all were gifts from God. My bones didn't hurt any less, and I wasn't any stronger. But I had been shown love and support; I had been comforted in a time of need.

I felt as if God had notified my friends and set up all these wonderful acts of kindness. They were just simple little things, those simple little things that are the most important in our lives.

Had my friends just happened to think of me on a day when I felt terrible? Were these all coincidences? No, these "God things" were not coincidences, but, even if they were, I would still thank God for putting together all these coincidences in my life.

So many things happen in our lives that are from God and, for so many years, I— like most people—didn't see them. Or I ignored them or explained them away as coincidences. Until I truly tried living a faith-filled life, I never grasped the concept of His ever-present power.

Throughout my life, God has been with me. *I'm* the only difference in whether I see his presence or don't. The more I trust in Him, the easier life is. God is everywhere, and willing to help, and, the more I ask, the more He does. The more I look, the more clear He is. The more I listen, the more noise He makes.

ONLY GOD KNOWS

The Norton Community High School senior class was putting together the first baccalaureate ceremony to be held in many years, and I was so honored when they asked me to speak. The fact that this was Pam's graduating class made it even more special.

When the afternoon arrived, I talked about looking for God in everything and everyone. I told the graduates to be positive and to have dreams, and, when their dreams change or don't go the way they've planned, to then be thankful to God for helping them grow.

I tried very hard, with God's guidance and love, to have a real message for the kids, as well as making it humorous and enjoyable. I hoped they would be proud. After all, this speech was for them. I finished with their class motto, the motto of Matt Ward, my cousin's son and their classmate who had died years before. "Just do your best," I quoted, then added, "and God will do the rest."

Afterwards, a grade school boy ran up to give me a hug, and everyone seemed to enjoy my talk.

Nearly everyone, that is. A couple of so-called "Christians" expressed their displeasure, letting me know I hadn't talked enough about Jesus.

They obviously hadn't paid attention to my speech. After all, I had begun by encouraging people to look for the good in everything. Their looking for what I had done wrong was not what I was talking about.

More important, my understanding is that Our Father, the Son, and the Holy Spirit are One. My speech was based on Philippians 4:13—"I can do all things through Christ Who strengthens me"—and how God has helped my faith grow through all the challenges I have faced. I believed I *was* talking about Jesus.

We can all plant a seed, but it's not always done the same way. Some think you have to shove the Bible down people's throats, while others try to do it through guilt. Some of my friends even try to scare God into others. I simply try to live my life for God, to be an example, and to share when asked. I feel my way is the correct way for me, although the others' ways may be right for them, and I am not going to judge. They may help a lot of people with their methods, but I have to trust God and live with my methods. When I die, I have to answer for me.

I was very pleased with my talk as the kids seemed to be happy with it, but I felt sadness for those people who didn't enjoy it, and were critical and judgmental. Usually when I get upset about something, it brings on a sadness that causes me to pray more about the situation—not for any particular outcome, but for God's will to be done and accepted. And, as always, God takes care of and comforts me.

Within a few days of my baccalaureate speech, I received the nicest letter from Pastor Lew, the local United Methodist minister. He wrote, "I felt the presence of Christ in your message. . . . You can say 'Jesus' a thousand times and not experience His presence." Some people understand my message; others don't. I have no control over either.

THOSE IN THE AUDIENCE

Many times during speeches, I find myself being drawn toward people in the audience as I sense their pain. For example, one evening I felt drawn toward an elderly woman at the rear of the auditorium. When I finished, I walked back to introduce myself. I was shocked when she told me her son—my age—had died just a few days earlier. We talked for several minutes as she expressed her pain.

If I had not paid attention to God's guidance, I would probably not have talked to this woman who had lost her son. I didn't have any answers for her. I couldn't fix anything. But I could listen compassionately, comfort her, and show my love.

During another speech, to some troubled youth, I kept being drawn toward a young man who looked like he was bored and wanted to be somewhere else. That's always possible, but I continued to talk, and to look at him more than anyone else. When I finished, he hurried to be the first one to where I stood, and said, "Sir, you inspired my heart. Thank you." My belief that he was bored made me focus more on him, and I knew God had been guiding me.

I spoke another time to a group of women, and felt drawn toward two of them, one to my left and one to my right, both near the front of the crowd. After my talk, I headed first to the lady on my right. She had just found out she had cancer and was beginning chemotherapy the following week.

The woman to my left, Michelle, had just lost her parents to different illnesses, four months apart, and I knew immediately we were supposed to meet. After visiting a few minutes, Michelle asked if I would speak at her church and to her Sunday School class.

When I spoke at her church, Michelle and her Sunday School students sang the most beautiful song, "When You Believe." She then very nicely introduced me by saying, "I recently read a quote from Albert Einstein saying you can live life in one of two ways. You can live life as if nothing is a miracle or you can live life as if everything is a miracle, and I believe Ward lives his life as if everything is a miracle."

After sharing my story and faith with the congregation, I greeted people at the back of the church, including an elderly man with a long white beard. He told me how much he enjoyed my talk, then asked if he could sing me a song. I was happy to listen to his beautiful song of praise to our Lord. When he finished, he said, "I am not the best singer, but wanted to give you something." This man and his song touched me more than I can put into words.

I spent the rest of the day relaxing with Michelle and her husband, Ken, until the time came for me to give another talk to some high school kids from local churches. I enjoy greatly being able to share my faith in church, but especially with kids. Part of me has never grown up, and this allows me to reach youth on their level.

OPINIONS

Driving home at the end of the day, I turned on the radio to enjoy some Christian music. However, once the music ended, the hosts began attacking, making fun of, and mocking people they didn't agree with—a politician, a movie star, even a religious figure.

I am saddened when someone "of God" attacks others and convicts them of sin for their beliefs and choices. We will be judged as we judge others. When I die, no one is going with me. Not my wife, not a priest or minister, not a friend or a sibling. No one is going with me. It is my responsibility to be right with God.

"Some 'Christian' station," I thought as I turned off the radio. I find it hard to believe people call themselves "Christian" when they spend their day attacking others. How does a "Christian" get away with saying such evil things about his brothers and sisters?

At least when I turn on Rush Limbaugh, I know he is a Republican and can't stand Democrats. I know Al Franken will attack Republicans. I can choose because I know what I am listening to.

But this "Christian" station was contradicting itself. The songs were speaking about God and love while the hosts were attacking everything and everyone they didn't agree with.

Another example of this occurred when Doug, a local attorney, was running for state representative. A week before the primary, a self-named "coalition" made known information about each candidate, some of which I felt was misleading. I immediately called Doug's secretary to ask what was going on. This took place so near to the election that Doug didn't even have enough time to respond. Deception is a nice word for what I feel this "church group" did. In politics, nothing surprises me; in our society, nothing surprises me. But I had hoped our churches would act in a different way. A church group is not a political group, but a faith organization. Of all places, I would think churches would be where we would find truth. Yet again, however, we humans have personal agendas.

Over many centuries every religion has been guilty of ungodly acts.

These acts were not performed by God or even the religion itself, but rather the human leaders of the church. As a society, I would hope we learned lessons from this history. We should not let religion get in the way of our faith. It should be the water that feeds our faith not the river that impedes us from reaching our faith on the other bank. Religion should help us love not keep us from loving by teaching us to hate.

Opinions are wonderful, and disagreeing is fine. This is how we learn from, and understand, others. But being hurtful and mean is not of God. I admire religious leaders who understand we are all of God, and are willing to go outside their denominations to help others. In hospice work, many times we call on these leaders to help patients, and I have yet to hear one say no, even when the person dying may not ever have attended their church. Among our local church leaders, Pastor Lew, Father Vincent, and Pastor Jeff are just a few with whom I have personally worked. All have gone beyond their denominational boundaries to help when I've asked. Each and every one has brought love and nonjudgmental attitudes toward these patients.

Jeff is the pastor of a Christian Church, and he and I disagree on a lot of issues. Yet his door is always open for me to enter and discuss these differences. He is a big reason my faith continues to grow stronger.

God has given all of us minds; using them is up to us. I often see people going to church and accepting everything they are told, never asking questions or thinking on their own. At times, doing hospice work, I have seen the most devout churchgoers struggle. They had accepted everything the church had taught them, but, as they were dying, where was the church? They had attended church regularly, given money, and even volunteered. They had a great relationship with their church. Many were caught up in living for the church, not God. They lacked the peace and the grace of God and a relationship with Jesus that no one but themselves could grasp.

Thank God, before these patients died, they discovered what it was all about, and finally enjoyed these gifts from God. It is so beautiful to see that peace in others, but I always wish it had come earlier in their lives. When God is in the center of a person, love is truly seen, and it pours into their world.

Accepting church rules with no thought of our own is dangerous. Accepting that the leader of a certain religion is always right, is wrong. "Thy will be done" doesn't mean my will be done, or someone else's will for me to be done. I can read the Bible myself, be filled with the Holy Spirit, and God can talk to me as easily as He can anyone else. I pray every day for God's guidance and direction. I read and study the Bible often. Would God lie to me or deceive me? Obviously, He would not. But He will lead us on different paths, enabling each of us to fulfill our journey to Him. I could never physically walk like a "normal" person, so I don't know why we think our spiritual walks will all be the same.

Two of us can read the same Bible and have a totally different perception and understanding. Who is right and who is wrong? The fact is, we both may be right. And does it really matter? Most Christian churches and religions agree on the basic core issues, beginning with Jesus and with love. The problems and confusion begin when we leave love, as that takes us away from Jesus. When we have to be right, our ego and pride get in the way. Too many people manipulate the Bible to fit their lifestyles. I simply believe in Jesus's most basic teaching—love thy neighbor. We of faith should be an example of what this means, and live together with love and acceptance.

We are each other's gifts, and, yet, many times we fail to recognize one another. Many times when we do not agree, we judge or attack instead of love. We feel our opinions are correct; thus everyone else's are wrong. Humans often do this in regard to their church and its beliefs. When I see people "of God" get angry at others for their beliefs, I ask, "Where is your peace?"

In my opinion, with this behavior, many people are putting a barrier between themselves and God's true love. People are being robbed because they have to be right. And when we allow the anger and attacks of others to infect us with anger and frustrations, we too shut ourselves off from God's unconditional love.

Letting others affect our walk only causes us to stumble, and, although I limp most of the time, my walk with God is becoming effortless. Living with peace, grace, and His love, I can allow people in my life to disagree with, judge, or criticize me, and it is fine, for only God knows the prayers and faith of a righteous man.

MY LUCKY SCARS

I know many people read the last chapter of a book first, so I originally had planned to end this book in the second-to-last chapter and make the final chapter a fictitious—and, I hoped, humorous—account of how I had won the Nobel Peace Prize. I told Donna about this idea, and she said, "No, don't do that." I asked why not, and she said, "Because I read the last chapter first, and I wouldn't think it was funny."

So this last chapter ends not with a "big bang," but with God.

One day I drew a picture of myself, an outline of my body, onto a piece of paper. I then added, in red, all my scars from all the surgeries and accidents. Once all the scars were shown, I erased the outline, and there I was. All the scars, from my toes to the top of my head, created a picture of me I called Scarman.

I then drew more pictures, each one with Scarman playing a different sport, and had them put on T-shirts, with appropriate sayings. For example, Scarman playing golf read, "Scarman has no handicap," and Scarman playing baseball read, "Scarman is a hit." A friend made Scarman dolls that I could donate to kids having surgeries. The Dane G. Hansen Museum, in Logan, Kansas, even honored me as one of their Artists of the Month.

I didn't make any money off these shirts. (Or, I should say, my parents and wife didn't get their money back from these shirts.) But creating them was a lot of fun and another way I could reach young people. Most important, however, was my own discovery of how far I had come in my acceptance of, and even pride in, my scars.

Throughout my life, I have always felt God's love. I was aware of it some times more than others, but, as my friend Steve once told me, it was never God who had left, only I who had turned away. Even during my worst times, however, I would cry out to God and, sure enough, He was there.

So, how is it that I could go through all that I have and yet be at peace? Why? According to some people, when bad things happen, it's God's fault.

How can I have as much faith as I do? Do I know something that many others don't? I think often of the gentleman who said I had been born less fortunate but now the strength of my faith made him feel less fortunate.

Why do I have what so many want? An acquaintance once said to me, "I want that peace and contentment you have. Can you give it to me?" It was as if it were just some "magical thinking," and I had a magic wand.

WHY?

My Uncle Iril told me once, that, when he had first seen me as a newborn, badly crippled and covered in plaster, he wondered how God could do that, or let it happen, to a little baby. Being that little baby, forty-five years later, now I can ask God those same questions, and more. God, did you do this to me? Did you let this happen to me?

Did you let those people call me a cripple, Frankenstein, and Monkey Ward? Sticks and stones may break your bones, but those names, they did hurt me. All I wanted was to be normal, to be like everyone else.

Did you allow those kids constantly to imitate and embarrass me when I walked through the halls every day at school? I hated going to school because of that ridicule.

Did you let those people point, stare, and laugh at me? I could walk through a mall and, as people passed by, without looking I could tell which ones were still staring and laughing. At times I felt so alone, and that no one understood me. I would have given anything not to be so skinny.

My dad used to put me through my exercises up to ten times a day. He bent my knees so far the pain was unbearable. It was as if he wouldn't quit until I was crying. And those horrible braces made me scratch my legs until they bled.

I had to struggle to do everything. Getting dressed, eating, even lifting a glass of water to my mouth—all was an effort. Why did everything in my life have to be so difficult? I cried myself to sleep so many times, suffering from physical and emotional pain.

All those first dates that never happened, and all those girls who just wanted to be friends? I've screamed, yelled, and even cursed.

The surgeries, and all those needles—why? It seemed I spent more time in the hospital than at home. I did enjoy missing school, but rehabilitation just caused more pain. My legs and arms still ache more often than they don't, and others still think I walk funny.

How could you let me fall in the fryer? Every day that Mom cleaned my hands, I screamed in agony. Those burns were excruciating.

Then, just when I thought I was finally doing well, why the drunk driver? I was so scared. Had I not been through enough?

Why did I have to get beat up? Not only did it hurt, but caused another surgery, and I still get headaches several times a week.

Every day of my life it seems I have encountered hurt, sadness, loneliness, and frustration. Why?

THIS IS WHY

I had learned that, no matter how bad things get, they can get worse. But they can also get better. To rephrase Murphy's Law, what can go wrong can also go right. While doctors were reconstructing my body through surgeries, God was watering and feeding my soul through the troubles and obstacles of life.

For my Uncle Iril and me, and all who wondered if God did this or let this happen to me, I can now say, "Thank you, Lord." I thank you, God, for teaching and walking with me even when I screamed, yelled, cursed, and questioned.

All those people who teased and laughed at me? Thank you, Lord, for teaching me compassion, empathy, and understanding. Now, someone in despair listens intently, hanging on every word I say, just because of what I've been through. All that pain has enabled me to bring them hope. Thank you, God, because now I can be there for other people during their hard times, and I can help You answer their prayers.

Thank you for teaching me patience. Thank you for giving me courage, strength, and determination. Thank you for teaching me forgiveness and the true meaning of love. Thank you for helping me trust in you. Thank you for blessing me with your grace and peace. Thank you for the joy I have known, and for helping me grow into the happiest person I know.

Thank you for my father's hard work, even when he made me cry. I am able to walk because of his love. Thank you for all the operations, and thanks, Lord, for keeping me in stitches, literally and figuratively. Thank you for not allowing my face to land in the fryer. Thank you for sending the lady in white to help me when I was scared and thought I might die.

Thank you for my mother and father; for Kirk, Craig, and Chris; for Dr. Boutin; for Donna, Charlie, and Pam. Thank you for my aunts and uncles, nieces and nephews, good friends, and all those you have put in my path. Those pieces to the puzzle of my life fit perfectly.

Thank you for allowing me to see the peace in Glenn.

All those prayers people have said for me since the day I was born have been answered. Thank you, Lord, for giving me the gift of faith and then strengthening it throughout my life. Looking for the good and God in everything becomes a habit, with trust in Him. It is written, "Where I am weak, He is strong."

Now, why do I see what I see and feel what I feel? Just maybe because I pray daily and love God, knowing "I can do all things through Christ Who strengthens me." Just maybe because I suffered a great deal and continued to trust and believe in Him. Just maybe because Jesus did die for our sins and there truly is a God who loves and cares about my well-being.

MEANING IN SUFFERING

One night while I was writing this chapter, I found myself wide awake at 2:30 or 3:00 A.M., unable to sleep because of pain. My arms were aching and I couldn't get comfortable. I tried lying on the couch and that didn't help. A little frustrated, I asked God if there was a reason I wasn't sleeping. Then I turned on the television, began flicking through the channels, and came across the beginning of a program by Fr. Robert J. Spitzer, president of Gonzaga University, entitled "Suffering."

Incredible! This was an immediate answer to my question. For thirty minutes I heard, from a religious perspective, how I ended up where I am. I was amazed at how I had lived my life, with help from many others, while growing and finding that peace and God's love. I lived with God, and His help led me to the very place Father Spitzer talked about.

For example, Father Spitzer said that if we find meaning in our suffering, it can be positive. He also said to use suffering to find deeper meaning and greater purpose in our walk toward the kingdom of God. Love your weakness, he said; love your vulnerability and your need because they are the means through which you will learn of your dependence on God's love in all things. To open oneself to God is an act of humility which leads to love. Purely and simply, the act of surrendering to God will become your joy forever, if it's freely chosen. Such an act will bring us to the heights in the dignity of the love to which God has called us from the beginning of the world. And that is why St. Paul tells us, "In my weakness is my strength."

I was so amazed at what I heard and saw that I called to thank Father Spitzer and ask him if I could use some of what he said in my book. Not only did he say yes, but he spent more than twenty minutes helping me to an even greater understanding of God's love and the gifts I have received through the pain I have endured. Father Spitzer himself was another one of those many gifts.

When someone hurts us intentionally, who really is hurt? If we let such hurts destroy us, *we* lose, for nothing we do or think is going to affect the ones who hurt us. But if we lovingly forgive those who hurt us, then we are set free.

The drunk driver and the kids who beat me up are in no way affected by my feelings of hate, and hating these people accomplishes nothing for me. Rather, forgiving them, and trying to love them, frees me from anger and fills me with God's grace. Only one person can take away my peace, love, and faith—all gifts from God—and *I* am that person. If I live wanting pity, always whining and saying, "Poor me," I am choosing sadness. I am finding excuses and allowing others to control my life and my closeness to God. Loving your enemy is one of the hardest things to do and yet one of the most rewarding in God's eyes. Those who are hardest to love are the ones we need to try hardest to love.

When someone mocks me or my beliefs, then, why should I be upset? When someone disagrees with me, why should I get angry? If I am right with God, I should truly be at peace.

Many times we try and make ourselves feel better the wrong way. Yet I have *never* read in the Bible that Jesus did anything to hurt someone. Attacking someone is wrong, and stretching the truth is a lie. No judgments, no anger, no hatred—just love. No agenda, no lies, no deceiving—just love.

Gossiping can provide a small example of how we do something negative and against God in our everyday lives that causes nothing but pain and pulls us from His love. I often remind myself how God can make good out of bad by replacing the word "gossip" with the acronym, "**G**o **O**ut, **S**it **S**ilently, **I**n **P**rayer." If I go out and sit silently in prayer, I come closer to God instead of farther away.

I do not have all the answers (even though I make my kids think so). I can't and don't try to figure out why all things happen, although I may ask. I just try to accept and love God, knowing He will bring me closer and lead me down the road that's best for me.

I still get sad and lonely and have bad days, and, like everyone, I make a lot of mistakes. I have hurt and disappointed people. I have made a lot of wrong decisions and will continue to do so through the rest of my life. My cousin Jimmy reminded me the other day that there is only one Jesus, and the rest of us just keep trying.

Yet, no matter how bad or stupid I have been, or what mistakes I have made, He died for all our sins. I will keep trying, keep praying, and keep trusting in Him. Each day is new, and I will wake up each morning (and from my afternoon nap), thanking the Lord for what I have. I'll keep trying to put on a smile, listen to Him, seek to do His will, live for Him, make Him proud.

MEANING IN DYING

I feel we cannot truly live until we face our own mortality. Many stay far away from death and those who are dying. Too depressing, too sad, they might think.

But eventually we will all be dying. Are we at peace? Are we ready for the next journey? I see so many people searching in all the wrong places, running in different directions, and, many times, crashing into one another. God's guidance toward peace and love has given me the strength I've needed. The road hasn't always been smooth. Sometimes there have been roadblocks or detours, and sometimes a mountain directly in the path, yet, with God, we can overcome all of life's obstacles.

And all encounter different obstacles in our journeys through life. So we can be thankful for what we do have, or we can be angry, focusing always on what we don't have. It's our choice. As my friend told me, God doesn't give us a good life or a bad life; He gives us life, and it is up to us to make it good or bad. We can thank Him or be angry—our choice. We can love or hate—our decision. Whichever we choose, the love comes from God.

I cannot give to others what I have, but I would like everyone to have it. Many people discover this true love of God only on their deathbeds, and I can only pray that everyone would discover it sooner. And it all begins with love, total love.

God is love beyond any human understanding. Imagine the most love you have ever felt and that is only a speck of what God's love is. The more I pray to God, the more I am filled with love; the more love I have, the more of God I want; the more I pray and ask for guidance, the more I am guided and led to His grace. Total peace and love are ours for the asking.

I mentioned to a friend once that I feel so close to God when I am with a hospice patient. The presence of His love is so strong in that situation, that love just fills the room. I jokingly said, if I ever needed a letter of reference, the only two who could give me one are God and the patient who died. The truth is, I try to love for God, and no one knows my heart but the patient and Him. I feel a dying patient is like a child who sees things many of us can't, literally and figuratively. When a patient is so close to God and His love, they see so much love in others and the truth in everyone. When I enter a patient's room with love, they see only the good in me and the love I have.

And the more we trust in Him, the easier the dying process is. Imagine if you suddenly had all the answers. You'd relax and be calm, as everything in life would make sense. Through faith in God, we can acquire all the answers of life, and those answers begin, again, with His love.

THE MEANING IN MY LIFE

When I was a child, my mother used to say, "The world doesn't revolve around you." Now my wife says it to me! In a sense, they're right. But, when I try to live with God, the world does revolve around me, and that should be true for each of us. In my little world, I can make a difference.

God created each of us, and no two of us are alike. We each choose the world in which we want to live, a loving world or a hateful world, as what we give is what we get, and our perception of all things is up to us. If we choose to hate, our life is miserable and so is the world we live in. But if we choose to love God and others, we will begin to see the love in the world, our world. In my world, I will continue to walk with God—or limp with the Lord—and live for the joys that come from the littlest and simplest of things.

I will thank God for the joy that comes when I visit a lady who cannot see and, yet, says so sweetly and softly as I walk into her room, "Is that you, Wardie?"

I will thank God for the joy that comes when I wave across the hall at a ninety-year-old woman and she waves back with a smile so bright, it could light up a night sky.

I will live for the joy that comes when a disabled child cries tears of thankfulness just because I spent a few minutes with him.

I will live for the joy that comes from reading the Bible for five minutes to someone because they asked, and praying with a lady who does not even remember my name.

I will live for the joy that comes when I give a friend a ride to the doctor, teach a child how to hit a baseball, or make young people laugh.

I will live for the joy that comes from sitting and sharing stories with a dying patient, or just "being there."

Mother Teresa said, "It is not how much we give, but how much love we put in the giving, that matters most." Young or old, rich or poor, black or white, gay or straight, doesn't matter when we talk about love, the love of God. We are to love everyone as if they are the most important person in the world.

I will put out my hand—no matter what it looks like—to love others, all others. I will continue listening and trying to follow God's will. I will do speeches when asked, visit residents at the nursing home, and, through hospice, will, God permitting, try to help dying people go peacefully. I will do what I can to help kids play baseball, I will teach Sunday School, I will even run errands for my wife, all while trying to keep a smile on my face.

I will live for the gifts: God's gracious gifts that begin with giving. People in our lives are gifts. Yet, no matter how many friends we have, all we really have is God.

I am not in the movies or on television, and I will never be famous. Yet, in God's eyes, I am already a star.

I haven't won the lottery and become a millionaire, but, with His love, I am the richest person alive.

I will never have my jersey retired or be a professional athlete on a cereal box, but I've been able to throw away my braces, and He has made me a champion.

I hope someday someone will see in me what I saw in my friend Glenn—God's love, God's peace.

There is no great ending to my story, and yet, this ending *is* the greatest. I prayed throughout childhood to be normal, to be just like everyone else, and I am.

I am Ward, just another person living an average life. I am no better and no worse. I am just like everyone else. I don't know what the future holds, but, whatever it is, I'm ready.

It is so easy to thank God for all the love and wonderful experiences

I have had throughout my life. Yet, it has been the hardships, struggles, and obstacles that have helped strengthen my faith and brought me closer to Him.

Each and every scar that I have, those that can be seen and those that can't, have made me who I am.

So I thank the Father, the Son, and the Holy Spirit, because, now, I can honestly say, "I thank my lucky scars."